"How can you make a brand synonymous with leadership, intelligence, and integrity? Karen Leland answers these questions and more with insight, warmth, and wit. This is a book that will help you raise your profile and turn heads."

—JOHN PAUL ROLLERT, HARVARD EXTENSION SCHOOL

"Every executive should read *The Brand Mapping Strategy*. It will open their eyes to what their full potential is, transform how they portray themselves, open doors to opportunities they aspire to, and ultimately inspire their teams and organizations to perform and achieve for a higher purpose."

—NINA LUALDI, SR. DIRECTOR OF LATAM INNOVATION CISCO

"From the personal to the corporate, from large organizations to small, *The Brand Mapping Strategy* is a critical market advantage for the bold and ambitious."

—ALAN WEISS, PH.D., BESTSELLING AUTHOR OF *MILLION DOLLAR CONSULTING*

"With characteristic wit, charm, and relatable anecdotes, Karen Leland's *The Brand Mapping Strategy* swiftly whisks the reader through the steps necessary to establish themselves and their business not only as a thought leader, but a true leader. This is an important read for anyone building a business, with something to say, or who desires to be truly heard."

—BINTA NIAMBI BROWN, *FORTUNE* MAGAZINE'S 40 UNDER 40 AND FOUNDER OF BIG MOUTH RECORDS AND FERMATA ENTERTAINMENT

"In this fast-changing, highly competitive era, it's more important than ever to know who you are and express it with distinction. Karen Leland's *The Brand Mapping Strategy* clearly and powerfully shows today's CEO how to create a personal brand that has a dramatic impact not only on their reputation, but the reputation of their companies."

—Ken Dychtwald, Ph.D., Bestselling author of *Age Wave*

"Building a personal brand is one of the essential skills for survival now and in the future. In *The Brand Mapping Strategy*, Karen Leland has provided a roadmap for every entrepreneur and CEO that is looking to master his or her brand, and turn it into a profitable competitive advantage."

—Stewart Emery, International bestselling author of *Success Built to Last*

"Karen Leland's *The Brand Mapping Strategy* is a must read for any C-level executive. It is full of practical advice for any leader looking to enhance their executive presence and transform their team."

—Marjorie Hutchings, CIO of State Fund Insurance

"*The Brand Mapping Strategy* has taken the mystery out of branding and provides a roadmap for any small-business owner, entrepreneur, or CEO to dramatically elevate both their personal and company brands."

—Adam Markel, CEO of New Peaks, formerly Peak Potentials

"*The Brand Mapping Strategy* captures the heart of what it means to have an authentic brand and how to powerfully and profoundly get there. I highly recommend it!"

—Lynne Twist, Bestselling author of *The Soul of Money*

"*The Brand Mapping Strategy* is an exceptional book for those who truly want to build effective brands, rather than just talk about it. Candid and practical, Karen Leland's emphasis on a research-based approach to brand building is a valuable guide for executives at every level."

—NATHAN RICHTER, PARTNER AT WAKEFIELD RESEARCH

"In *The Brand Mapping Strategy*, Karen Leland provides insider secrets to creating a world-class brand. Leaders will be inspired to transform not only the expression of their own brand, but that of their team and company."

—OLIVIA FOX CABANE, AUTHOR OF *THE CHARISMA MYTH*

"No matter what business you are in you don't just read *The Brand Mapping Strategy* study it and use it as your personal tool to set yourself, your company, and product apart from the pack."

—DAVE AUSTIN, INTERNATIONAL BESTSELLING AUTHOR OF *BE A BEAST*

"Karen Leland's dynamic and no-nonsense perspective clearly outlines how to effectively put your personal brand into action using visual, intellectual, and emotional capital! The step-by-step insights and guidelines she shares on how to differentiate yourself as a brand and enhance your brand equity are spot on and essential in today's ultra-competitive world of branding. A must read for anyone who wants to stand out amongst the clutter by creatively promoting their brand attributes and relevantly communicating their full brand potential!"

—THOMAS W. MERCHANT, FORMER INTERNATIONAL MARKETING & COMMUNICATIONS MANAGER OF PEUGEOT AUTOMOBILES, PARIS, FRANCE

The
Brand
Mapping
Strategy

Design
Build
and Accelerate
Your Brand

Karen Tiber Leland

Entrepreneur
PRESS®

Entrepreneur Press, Publisher
Cover Design: Andrew Welyczko
Production and Composition: Eliot House Productions

Library of Congress Cataloging-in-Publication Data
Names: Leland, Karen, author.
Title: The brand mapping strategy: design, build, and accelerate your brand / by
    Karen Tiber Leland.
Description: Irvine : Entrepreneur Press, 2016.
Identifiers: LCCN 2016007150| ISBN 978-1-59918-589-7 (paperback)
    | ISBN 1-59918-589-X
Subjects: LCSH: Branding (Marketing) | Marketing—Management.
    | Entrepreneurship. | Management—Technological innovations.
    | BISAC: BUSINESS & ECONOMICS / Entrepreneurship.
Classification: LCC HF5415.1255 .L445 2016 | DDC 658.8/27—dc23
LC record available at http://lccn.loc.gov/2016007150

Printed in the United States of America

20 19 18 17 16   10 9 8 7 6 5 4 3 2 1

For my late father, Dr. Norman Tiber—a great tango dancer and an even better teacher.

Contents

CHAPTER TWO

The Marketing Mastery Pyramid: *The Path to Industry and Thought Leadership* 13

CHAPTER THREE

The Brand Mapping Process©: *Seven Core Elements of a Powerful Business, Team, and Personal Brand* 31

CHAPTER FOUR

The Brand Mapping Strategy: *Creating Your Business and Personal Branding Plan*. 69

PART TWO
Your Personal Brand in Action

Acknowledgments

I t would be impossible to write an acknowledgments page for this book that accurately reflects all the people in my life who have ultimately contributed to its creation. Fortunately, you know who you are, so I can rest easy with just a few specific shout-outs:

- Jillian McTigue, Jennifer Dorsey, Vanessa Campos, and Karen Billipp at Entrepreneur Media. It's always a joy to work with such pleasant professionals.
- Nell McPherson, for always making sure my commas are in the right place.
- Anne Christine Strugnell, my fellow scribe and dear friend, who sat with me for hours on end tapping away on our laptops, sipping tea, and stopping to laugh and eat chocolate at appropriate intervals.

- Susan Harrow, Liza and Raz Ingrasci, Les and Irving Bernstein, Monica Norcia, Kim Bromley, Jennifer Reimer, Caryn and Ron Rosenberg, Deborah Coffey, Colleen Rudio, September Dohrmann, Theresa and Don Souers, Maggie Weiss, Randy Roberts, Dr. Alyse Danis, Carla Madison, Barbara Tiber, Anne Tiber, and Sheila Vasan Singla, for being there in good times and bad.
- Finally, to my clients at Sterling Marketing Group, thank you for allowing me to support you in bringing your messages out into the world. I feel deeply honored to be entrusted with your brands.

The Power of Conscious, Authentic Branding

O ver a nine-month period between the summer of 2013 and spring of 2014, I separated from my husband of 22 years, moved from San Francisco to New York, started a new romance and ended it heartbroken, moved back to San Francisco, and filed for divorce. Shortly after, my mother's husband passed away after a long illness, and two weeks later, my father unexpectedly died of a stroke.

That was not a good year. But the silver lining was that it brought about a forced rebrand in my personal life that had been a long time in coming. The person I knew myself to be was in many ways gone, and two of the roles I had held dear (my father's daughter and someone's wife) disappeared almost overnight. This left me disoriented, but with a life-changing sense of vulnerability.

Over the next two years, I consciously worked to grieve and eventually to reinvent my life (and my personal brand) from an authentic place that reflected who I had become. The inner work I did naturally spilled over and significantly reshaped my business brand.

Along the way, I gained a whole new insight into and appreciation for the power of authentic and conscious branding—be it business, team, or personal. This understanding has transformed my work with CEOs, senior executives, and entrepreneurs and their businesses, organizations, and teams. The book you now hold in your hands (or on your tablet) reflects what I have learned about creating the awareness, developing the vision, and implementing the strategy you need to organically move a personal and business brand to the next level.

TOP TEN REASONS TO BUY THIS BOOK

The people who will get the most out of this book share two attributes with my private clients: 1) They hope to bring their personal or business brands to that next level, and 2) they have a relentless desire to contribute their gifts to the world. If you bought this book, it's likely to be for one (or more) of the following reasons:

1. You want to expand your current brand outreach and contribution to a bigger audience in your industry, community, or the world at large.

2. You know you need to be head and shoulders above the crowd, sought after and seen as having high value, but you are not always sure how to navigate the branding, PR, and marketing waters to get there.

3. You want to be seen as a thought or industry leader, which requires clear positioning, a specific strategy for brand building (online and off), and a method for implementation—none of which you are sure how to achieve.

4. You are looking to establish a clearer, stronger, or different personal brand within your current company as a path to greater executive presence, promotion, or expanded opportunity.

5. You are so busy with the day-to-day needs of your company that you have not developed the knowledge to do the branding and marketing required to build your business.

6. You have tons of great content that could be better leveraged but are overwhelmed or confused as to how to effectively and efficiently get it out into the world and build your brand.

7. You believe it is time to rebuild, refine, reinvent, or rev up your personal or business brand, but you are not sure where to start or how to get there.

8. You feel overwhelmed or confused about what your marketing and social media strategy should be.

9. You realize you need to be well positioned online for career management, but you don't have the knowledge you need to maximize your online reputation.

10. You see competitors being touted as thought leaders and interviewed by the media and think, "That should be me."

HOW TO USE THIS BOOK FOR MAXIMUM BENEFIT

I happily spend most of my days at work helping CEOs, executives, and entrepreneurs develop stronger personal, business, and team brands. But like all entrepreneurs, my reach is limited by my capacity. I wrote *The Brand Mapping Strategy: Design, Build, and Accelerate Your Brand* as a way to touch all the people I won't ever have the privilege of meeting in person, but for whom this message is still important. With that in mind, there are a few ways that you, the reader, can use this book to gain maximum benefit for your brand.

Borrow a Lesson from the World of Hula

For several years I studied hula dancing in Hawaii. I was privileged enough to study under a revered, multigenerational kumu (teacher) of hula named Kawaikapuokalani Frank Hewett.

Frank has a sign hanging in his hula studio that reads "A'ohe pau ka 'ike i ka hālau ho'okahi," which translated into English means "All knowledge is not learned in just one school." This is as true in branding as it is in hula.

This book is the accumulation of the work I have done in this area over several decades. The ideas proffered here are not theoretical but rather come from my professional observations in the field working with everything from small businesses to Fortune 1000 companies, in 50 countries around the world, and in every industry you can imagine, from software and shipping to banking and baking.

While the ideas in this book have been proven over time with my clients, no single author or expert has the final say on what works in branding (hence the sign in Frank's hula studio). My best advice to you in using this book is to take what you like and leave the rest.

Don't Be Afraid to Go Modular

This book was intentionally written in segments so that you could find the parts in it that are the most important to you at this time. Although I strongly suggest reading Part One first to get a foundational understanding of your business or personal brand, each chapter stands on its own.

In addition, I've given many real-life examples throughout the book to help you see how these ideas translate into practical reality. *One note*: In most cases my clients and the people I mention or interview have given me permission to use their real names and company names. In those cases where using a real name was not an option I have changed the name of the client but kept the circumstances of the situation factual.

Finally, keep in mind that this book is meant to be a companion you can customize on your branding journey.

- You may be in a particular pickle right now and need to use this book as an emergency measure.
- You may read this book from cover to cover in one sitting and with great gusto take all the actions recommended.
- Perhaps you will read one part, put the book down for a bit and implement it, and then pick it up again.
- This book may become a part of your yearly brand review.

- You and your team may use this book to transform the way you do business.

In any and all of these cases, and more, it's all about making this book work for you and your brand. Other than that, as your mother used to say, "just do your best," and call me if you have any questions.

Sincerely,
Karen Tiber Leland
Sterling Marketing Group
www.karenleland.com
San Francisco, California/New York City, New York

If you would like access to my blog, additional ideas, articles, ebooks, webinars, online training, and other free stuff and goodies on social media, marketing, and business, team, and personal branding, please visit me at www.karenleland.com, or contact me at Karen@karenleland.com.

PART ONE

Ready, Aim, Brand

The New Branding and Marketing Mindset and Myths

How to Brand Yourself and Your Business in the Digital Age

In its heyday, when *The Oprah Winfrey Show* was the holy grail of marketing, every new client would invariably ask, "Can you get me on *Oprah*?" They were all convinced that whatever they were hawking (everything from self-published books on CEO skills for daddies to a new and improved peanut butter) was a perfect fit for the queen of daytime television. If only they could reach that peak of media greatness, the magic would rub off and they would rake in millions. In reality, about 95 percent of them were not a good fit for the show and its audience. Regardless, clients still insisted, "My main goal is to be on *Oprah*."

Very few ever made the cut. In the first place, getting on the show was extremely difficult (the realm of the lucky few) and could take months, if not years. For those who did succeed in being booked (full disclosure: I was on as a guest expert based on one of my books), the show did not always turn out to be the panacea that cured all their promotional ills. Guests whose books and products were actually a perfect fit for the *Oprah* audience had strong results, but for others, it gave a boost to their credibility but did not necessarily translate into more business or higher sales.

I did some consulting with one bestselling author who was strongly leaning toward turning down interviews with several prominent media outlets simply because she was already scheduled to appear on *Oprah*. When I suggested that wasn't a strategically sound branding move, she retorted that she had been on the show with her first book, and as a result of "the Oprah Effect," it had become a hit.

"I understand your temptation to take this approach," I said, "but your first book was several years ago, and the internet and social media have changed things. The audience and the way people buy books have shifted."

Nonetheless, she insisted on focusing the vast majority of her book-branding efforts on Oprah and privately expressed to me a few months later how disappointed she was that it had not resulted in the flood of book sales and seminar enrollments she had expected.

In fact, her publisher—anticipating the Oprah windfall—had published a much higher than usual number of books for a first run. In the end, she did sell books from the *Oprah* appearances, but about 50 percent fewer than her publisher had planned for.

Fast-forward to today. *The Oprah Winfrey Show* is no longer on the air, and overall, a paradigm shift in branding and marketing has taken place. The most successful entrepreneurs, business owners, and individuals have set their sights on developing a long-term platform for brand and buzz building over time—instead of hoping for an overnight success.

That's really the key to the new branding (and marketing) mindset—the recognition that building a brand, be it personal, team, or business, is the result of an ongoing, steady stream of consistent small efforts, not a series of one-off, gigantic pushes.

As a branding and marketing consultant, I've observed three specific shifts in my field that every entrepreneur and executive needs to be aware of.

SHIFT 1: FROM THE LUCKY FEW TO THE PERSISTENT MANY

Social media has leveled the playing field and made obsolete the old mindset, which favored the lucky few. In other words, if you were fortunate enough to get written about in *The Wall Street Journal* or *The New York Times* (or appear on *Oprah*), you moved to the top of the press heap and considered yourself as having arrived. That was the old model.

Today, businesses (big and small) that are consistent in their branding are getting PR, buzz, and attention. It doesn't take a big, complicated marketing plan, but it does require a persistent approach to promotion.

Consider the world of book marketing. In the past, when an author would sign a book deal, a publisher would do all the legwork to promote the book. An internal PR department or external PR agency hired by the publisher would send out press releases and create a campaign to get exposure for the book and its author. The highest-profile authors (the lucky few) got the most PR support from the publisher, and the

---

Be Ubiquitous

In the past, you put your business, book, or product out there and hoped the media found you. Today you become ubiquitous in your field of expertise, and journalists and potential clients looking for experts find you. The goal is to become the haystack high up in the field, not the needle buried deep down in the pile. This new mindset is all about how your proactive efforts put the power and the possibilities of being known within your reach.

For example, I know one woman who almost died due to a severe soy allergy. Inspired by her experience, she began writing widely about the topic on food allergy forums, nutrition blogs, and other relevant online venues. After she had spent about a year consistently contributing via blogs, recipes, comment sections, etc., a reporter from *The New York Times* who was writing a story on the subject called wanting to interview her.

Since my client was neither a published book author nor a nutritionist, she was curious as to how the reporter had made the connection. "How did you find me?" she asked. "I Googled the topic, and your name came up everywhere," the reporter replied.

Chapter One • **The New Branding and Marketing Mindset and Myths**

larger pool of smaller fish received just a month or two of minimal PR support.

In the interest of getting their books sold, many authors hired a PR firm at their own expense to do additional publicity, which could cost them $20,000 to $40,000 for a four-month campaign. The results were all over the map, and once the four months were up, the book was not considered new or fresh enough to promote further—at least not with any intensity.

Today, many authors, whether their books are self-published or traditionally published, have taken book promotion into their own hands with the background support of PR firms, webmasters, online services, and marketing and branding consultants. The average self-managed campaign can be done on a budget of $12,000 instead of $20,000, and the window for promotion has grown from a few months to a few years (or more) for books whose topics are evergreen in nature.

Book promotion is no longer a sprint won by the lucky few but a marathon conquered by the persistent many—and at a lower cost.

The same holds true for small businesses and entrepreneurs. Those who are making themselves ubiquitous in their fields through the consistent use of content marketing, PR, speaking, and other brand-building strategies are getting noticed as the thought leaders in their industries.

SHIFT 2: FROM THE BIG STICK TO SMALL AND TARGETED

As with the *Oprah* example from the beginning of this chapter, another change in the branding and marketing mindset is that success is no longer the result of two or three big media hits. In the past, the goal was to be covered by a major magazine, newspaper, or TV program. Those hard-to-come-by hits were considered to make or break your business, book, or product.

Today, success doesn't hinge on a few hot hits to a huge audience but on hundreds or thousands of smaller ones targeted to just the right users for your brand. I find that for many entrepreneurs, experts, and executives, it's difficult to shift out of the old paradigm since the allure of the most popular, biggest, and best-known media outlets is so deeply ingrained.

I recently had a conversation with a woman who wanted blog reviewers for her new product launch only if they received monthly hits numbering in the millions. She didn't realize that a blog that gets 10,000 hits a month—but targets her ideal audience—was worth far more than a blog with millions of hits whose audience wasn't on the mark. Finding the right audience (small and targeted) instead of going for the one with the most viewers (the big stick) can make all the difference.

Be honest. If I asked you which you would prefer, a popular pin on Pinterest or an appearance on the *Today* show, which would you choose? I've put this question to thousands of people in my keynote speeches, and the vast majority raise their hands for *Today*. It's perfectly understandable but not always the right answer.

One of my favorite examples of this is entrepreneur Holly Xerri, owner of the online retail business Camibands. I learned Xerri's story when I interviewed her for my previous book, *Entrepreneur Magazine's Ultimate Guide to Pinterest for Business*.

In August 2011, Xerri was offered the opportunity to appear on *Today* to discuss her sartorial creation, the Camiband—a multipurpose wardrobe extender for women that acts as a cleavage cover, among other things.

The result of Xerri's appearance on the show was a happy 3,500 hits to her website and an influx of orders. In December of that same year, a week before Christmas, a huge flood of orders suddenly came in. Xerri checked and saw she had received 40,000 hits to her website over a four-day period. The source of those hits, according to Google Analytics? Users on Pinterest who had pinned images of the Camiband found on her site.

Xerri's brand was helped by being on *Today*, but it went viral via Pinterest—a social media site representing her exact audience. Eighty percent of Pinterest users are women between the ages of 25 and 54. According to an analysis by Shopify, Pinterest customers spend an average of $80 with each order, twice that of Twitter and Facebook customers. It may be a smaller audience than *Today*, but for Xerri it packed a bigger impact.

I'm not saying it's a bad thing to get booked on a major media outlet—it's terrific. If you can get word out about your brand on a known television, radio, or print media outlet, by all means do. I always aim to get my clients the "big" hits. I just don't make the mistake of thinking:

1. It's all you have to do.
2. It's the only way to go.
3. It's always going to produce the best results.

If you recognize the value of the big hits for what they are—great leveraged credibility for your brand by association—then you win, even if they don't drive huge traffic to your site or inspire customers to knock down your door.

Today, you don't have to wait for "the big sticks" of media to deem your work worthy of attention. You will be much more successful if you aim your brand building at smaller venues that attract the perfect audience for you, instead of that one giant hit. Just remember: Getting in front of a huge audience won't grow your business if it's the wrong audience for you.

SHIFT 3: FROM A SPRINT TO A MARATHON

A potential client recently asked me, "What conversion rate can I expect over the next few weeks in terms of new business if we put out this press release?"

"That's the wrong question," I said. "The value of the release can't and shouldn't be measured by short-term conversion rates alone."

Press releases, social media, blogging, and other content-marketing and business-development activities—both online and off—are about the persistent, ongoing process (a marathon) of building a platform, creating credibility, and increasing the number of people you funnel into your potential client pipeline or network. They are not about a quick sprint toward a short-term outcome.

Converting the people you have funneled into your pipeline into clients, fans, or connections may take weeks, months, or years, but this new mindset leads you to strategies that will keep that pipeline full. In short, you need to start and maintain a bunch of small fires to keep your brand burning hot. Here's an example from my own business.

Years ago I wrote a marketing article for my then-column in *The Huffington Post*. I got paid nothing to write it, and honestly, I don't even remember the specific topic. Regardless, it must have struck a chord with at least a few people, because I received an email from a reader saying she had enjoyed the post and thought I should connect with a media trainer named Susan Harrow.

At the time I had no idea who Susan was, so I looked her up on the internet. We seemed to have some professional crossover, and she looked interesting enough, so I sent her a LinkedIn invitation.

One side note here: Whenever I reach out to someone online who does not know me, I like to include a link to my LinkedIn profile as well as a few articles I've written or that have been written about me. This is my way of saying, "I'm a legitimate businessperson and not some online nutter out to sell, harass, or hound you."

There is a whole lot of crazy out there, which has led to people being a bit hesitant when a message arrives in their inbox from someone they don't know, so it's important to establish your credibility early on. Part of the value of treating branding as a marathon is that you end up with an online history that validates who you are and where you have come from.

She must have liked what she saw (or at least it didn't scare her) because she accepted my LinkedIn request and sent me a to-the-point message saying, "I looked at your website, and I loved the vibrancy. Let's set up a time to chat by phone."

A week later we were on the telephone having a great conversation and discovered that we live in the same city—about ten minutes away from each other. What are the odds? Taking advantage of geography, we decided to meet for lunch.

Over pad Thai noodles and chicken satay (with extra peanut sauce), we continued to delight in our personal and work similarities. At the end of the meal, Susan looked at me with a gleam in her eye and said, "Let's order dessert." That's when I knew we'd be friends for life.

About a month later, Susan sent me a client referral. It was a small branding strategy project worth about $3,500. A few months later, that client called me saying they had a vendor who was looking for the type of work I did. That resulted in a six-month branding strategy and implementation project with a $30,000 price tag. For a period of two years, I kept track of all the business that came to me through Susan's referral, and her referral's referral. At last count it was $150,000.

What's in a Word?

I want to take a few seconds to discuss some of the terms I will be using throughout this book. Although this may drive the word perfectionists among you crazy, I am going to play a little fast and loose with language. Specifically I'm going to take creative license with the words

- Branding
- Marketing
- Promotion
- Public relations (PR)

Although the focus of this book is on designing, building, and accelerating a brand—be it personal, team, or business—in the world we live in, it's harder than ever to tuck these terms into a nice, neat bento box of business school terminology.

In real-world practice, branding, marketing, promotion, and PR work side by side in a coordinated effort. It's often hard to tell where one begins and the other ends. Take an example from one of my clients—Learning as Leadership (LaL), who offer personal mastery programs for executives of Fortune 500 companies.

I was working with CEO Shayne Hughes to craft a blog post for www.Forbes.com focusing on an experiment Shayne conducted where he banned email in the company for a week.

The post was popular and became number one on the www.Forbes.com site for a few days. This of course created an expanded awareness of the LaL brand, increased traffic to the company website, and enhanced LaL's social proof and credibility—all good.

A year later, Shayne was sitting in his office when he got a copy of Arianna Huffington's latest book, *Thrive*. It turned out that Ms. Huffington had seen

> ## What's in a Word?, continued
>
> Shayne's post on www.Forbes.com and included a reference to it (and LaL) in her book. How do you categorize that? Branding? Marketing? PR? I would say in reality it was a combination of all three. But whatever you call it, it was good for business.

My point is that we're so crazy busy trying to measure the immediate return we get on branding activities (be it social media or speaking at a conference) that we are missing out on the long-term impact of these actions. When I wrote that one little blog post (for free), I didn't know where it would lead. I had no expectation that it was going to do anything beyond increase my credibility. Ultimately it not only led to business, but to this day Susan is one of my closest friends and colleagues—and that is priceless.

Once you understand (and embrace) the powerful shifts in branding and marketing that are going on in today's digital world, you'll be itching to jump headlong into becoming a branding big shot in your field. Not so fast.

Several times a week I get a call from an exasperated entrepreneur or executive complaining about the money they've spent hiring someone in the web design, social media, branding, marketing, or PR space—who did not deliver what they expected or wanted.

Sometimes this is a function of poor hiring, but often it's a case of poor timing. In the rush to get in the game, business people regularly skip the preparation work necessary to make brand-building activities as efficient and effective as possible. The next chapter will introduce you to a specific path for achieving thought and industry leadership efficiently and effectively, one smart step at a time.

CHAPTER TWO

The Marketing Mastery Pyramid

The Path to Industry and Thought Leadership

Almost every entrepreneur, expert, and executive I encounter boldly declares, "I want to be a thought leader." My half-joking response: "Well, first you have to have some thoughts."

In other words, you can't just declare yourself a thought (or industry) leader. It doesn't happen because you say so—it happens because the world says so. In order to be a thought or industry leader, you need to rise to such a level of expertise or excellence that people (media, other industry leaders, clients, etc.) will seek you out as a recognized authority.

The big question is, how do you get there? The answer is that you need to engage in a branding process to legitimately position yourself at that level. The method I created to help my clients work their way through that process is the Marketing Mastery Pyramid (see Figure 2.1 on page 14)—a three-step

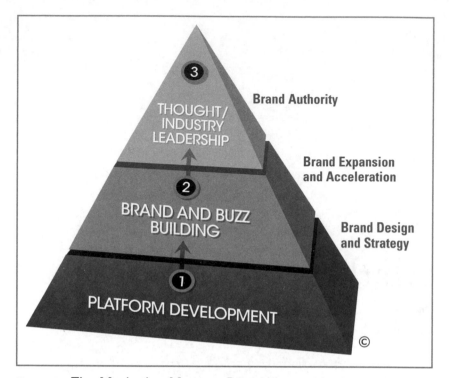

Figure 2.1: **The Marketing Mastery Pyramid**

journey that organically grows individuals and businesses from platform development through brand building and lands them squarely in thought/industry leadership.

I believe that fully understanding this process, including where the greatest pitfalls, challenges, and opportunities lie in each phase, is a critical first step in building a solid brand. The following is a bird's-eye view of each level. *One note*: As usual, I will be using a few words interchangeably to describe this process. The words *phase*, *level*, and *step* all express the same thing—the three stages we follow in order through the Marketing Mastery Pyramid to eventually arrive at thought/industry leadership.

At the end of the chapter, you'll have a chance to take a short quiz to determine where you currently are on the pyramid—and what you should do to move yourself and your company to the next level.

PHASE ONE: PLATFORM DEVELOPMENT—BRAND DESIGN AND STRATEGY

Phase One is all about developing a solid platform on which you can build your brand and market your business. It requires defining, articulating, and declaring your brand and then translating that into places (online and off) where people can effectively engage with your business. That probably doesn't come as news to you; however, if you are like many of my clients, your tendency is to move quickly past this first phase and jump headlong into the more exciting work of spreading the word.

The problem is that I have seen far too many people haphazardly rush into building buzz for their brand (Phase Two), only to drive traffic back to a website and/or social media sites that don't hit the mark. Whenever I speak at a conference, the most common statement I hear is "I'm spending all this money on PR and marketing, but I'm not getting the results I want for my efforts." In many cases, a big part of the problem is a lack of clarity about the brand as well as web and social media sites that are:

- Sloppy (bad writing, grammar, and spelling)
- Poorly designed (ugly and/or not user-friendly)
- Badly branded or lacking any brand feel at all
- Inconsistent in message and look
- Unclear in their brand message (vague, confused, unclear)
- Not using marketing best practices

The path to thought and industry leadership must start with a solid platform. Before you begin any PR, marketing, or buzz-building campaigns, three critical actions, taken in a specific order, are required:

1. First, clearly articulate your brand and messages.
2. Next, develop a modern, marketing-oriented, up-to-date website.
3. Finally, create brand consistency on social media.

Clearly Articulate Your Brand and Messages

Have you ever heard the expression "If I had a dollar for every time . . . ?" Well, here's my version. If I had a dollar for every time a businessperson has complained to me about the countless hours (and enormous amount of money) they have spent on building a website that wasn't quite right, I'd be retired in Hawaii watching the waves, a fruity drink in my hand.

Building a website before determining the specifics of your brand message is always a mistake. Your brand is what drives the website design—not the other way around. My mantra is "Brand Before You Build." The first thing to do when creating your platform—before you build a website or go all hot and heavy on any social media site—is establish a clearly articulated brand and messages.

The issue at this point becomes how that brand is defined. For many people, what comes to mind are the three Ls: look, logo, and line.

The look is the style and design elements of the brand (including colors, fonts, etc.), the logo is the symbol representing the business in the marketplace (be it a graphic image or typography), and the line is a few sentences (a tagline, an elevator pitch, etc.) that briefly describe both what the business is and what it does.

I often talk to business owners who tell me they are in the process of "rebranding." Upon further discussion, I discover that what they are really doing is changing the visual elements of their brand. Business people often rely (too heavily, in my opinion) on just a design change to move their brand to the next level.

Are the three Ls an important part of your brand? Without question. But they're only the tip of the iceberg when it comes to defining your message. You also need to take a deeper dive and articulate seven other core brand elements

These elements provide a deeper way to talk about and represent your brand. Chapter 3 will take you in detail through the Brand Mapping Process© and the seven core brand elements I've identified in my work with clients. These elements are:

1. Anchor Statement
2. Unique Branding Proposition
3. Brand Tone and Temperament
4. Brand Energy

5. Signature Story
6. Signature Services
7. Brand Enhancers and Reducers

You may be wondering, why seven core elements and not ten, or five? There are as many branding processes out there as there are branding consultants—and none of us have the final word or one right answer on how to get to the descriptive heart of a brand. But over the past decade, I've found these seven to be the most useful ones for my clients to define their personal and business brands.

Develop a Modern, Marketing-Oriented Website

Now that your brand is solidly defined, you're ready to move on to the next step in platform development—developing a modern, marketing-oriented, up-to-date website.

In my experience, many business people (especially entrepreneurs and small-business owners) grossly underestimate the impact and importance of their websites. I can tell you with absolute certainty that the quality of your website is critical to your customers, potential customers, and even members of the media. Here are two stories that illustrate this point.

THE DISAPPOINTED JOURNALIST

I recently had a conversation with a reporter from a major media outlet who was lamenting the lack of usable sources for stories. "I often get referred to an expert who I think would be a good interviewee for a piece I'm writing," she told me. "But when I go to their website, it is so badly written, designed, or simply unprofessional that I can't risk using them.

"If I quote them as an expert and a reader goes to their website and sees how poorly executed it is, that calls into question their credibility and as a result reflects badly on me," she explained. "It looks like I did not do my research and find a top-notch person to interview."

Personally, I found that fascinating—but not surprising. It was interesting that a credible expert can't be used because of their website's perceived lack of credibility. I wish I could say this was an unusual event in my line of work, but in fact it's a common occurrence.

THE CLUELESS DENTIST

In the same way a poor website can chase the media away, it can also keep potential customers at bay. One of my favorite examples is a dentist who called me for assistance in marketing and branding his practice. His essential problem was that even though he was the only dentist within a 60-mile radius offering a specialized cosmetic dental procedure, a competing dentist 90 miles away was getting a greater percentage of his potential clients.

He couldn't understand why, but one look at his website told me the whole story. His online presence was weak and his website sloppy. When I suggested this might be the problem, he retorted, "Oh, patients don't care about a website. It doesn't make any difference."

I told him that while I was not a dental marketing expert per se, I had strong doubts as to the accuracy of that statement and proposed we take a look at his competitor's website. I asked him to pretend he was a potential patient shopping dentists for the high-end cosmetic procedure he specialized in. "What would your first impressions be of this dentist, landing on just the home page of this site?" I asked.

"This guy is a total professional, knows what he is doing, and is worth the money," he said.

"OK. Let's go to the homepage of your website now," I suggested. "Remember, you are a patient looking for a dentist. First impressions?"

After a long pause, I met with a low grumbling. "This guy looks like a bit of a hack," he said.

Although both of these dentists had in reality roughly the same level of education, experience, and pricing, it was the one who looked more professional via his website who was converting online shoppers to paying patients.

I think you've got the point. The quality of your website matters. Although I'm not a web designer myself, I spend a good deal of my time wrangling them for clients to get their brands right.

There are hundreds of large and small decisions that impact how well a website reflects a business's brand and marketing orientation. The amount of advice about what you should do and how you should do it can be overwhelming. Just type "website design" into Google, and you will

The Truth Will Win Out

What the above stories illustrate is that in the internet age, being good (or even great) at what you do is unfortunately not enough. Looking good online has become a critical factor for success. The bright side of being able to establish a brand online is that it has both broadened and leveled the playing field. A business that was once too small to go up against a bigger competitor can now, via a keyword-rich web search, get noticed and hired by a potential customer.

The dark side? There are people out there who are not great, good, or sometimes even adequate at their vocations, but can seem so through effective branding. However, while the internet may allow a businessperson to hang out a shingle that claims "Awesomeness This Way," things usually seem to right themselves one way or another. A business can brand its way to success for only so long without delivering the goods before the market catches on and the internet becomes foe, not friend, to these mediocre practitioners.

Business review websites and apps (think Yelp, Angie's List, etc.) are gaining greater power every day over influencing consumer and company buying decisions.

According to a research report by Zendesk on how customer service impacts revenue (www.zendesk.com/resources/customer-service-and-lifetime-customer-value), 88 percent of people surveyed were influenced by an online customer service review when making a buying decision.

be rewarded with more than a billion results. Similarly, a search for "web design" returns tens of thousands of books and products.

All this is my way of saying that I could write a book on the topic of designing your website—but that's not the purpose of this one. So below is a very brief glance at just a few elements that I feel pack the biggest punch. And while they may seem obvious, every day I see websites that miss the mark on these basic items.

COLOR AND DESIGN

Specific colors and types of design (fonts, layouts, etc.) go in and out of fashion. What might have been considered modern a year ago seems dated today. The quintessential example is the 1980s top dog of color—mauve. At onc time it was the new black, found on everything from logos to living room walls. Today, mauve is mostly considered an old-fashioned hue— something your granny might wear.

One infographic from Kissmetrics (https://blog.kissmetrics.com/color-psychology/?wide=1) highlighted various research on the impact of color and design on online branding and buying, including the following points:

- Color increases brand recognition by 80 percent.
- 42 percent of shoppers base their opinion of a website on overall design alone.
- 52 percent of shoppers did not return to a website because of overall aesthetics.
- 93 percent of consumers place visual appearance and color above other factors when shopping.

It is statistics like these (and hundreds more) that leave me shaking my head in wonder when a business owner tells me, "I just left that stuff up to my web guy." While many web developers have a terrific feel for what looks good (and many don't), it's still critical for clients to think through the brand messages that certain colors, fonts, layouts, and other design elements evoke.

SPEEDY NAVIGATION

Let's face it: People have no patience. According to one survey by Kissmetrics (https://blog.kissmetrics.com/loading-time/?wide=1), web-sites with a mere one-second delay in page response time can see a 7 percent reduction in conversions. The bottom line is that your visitors won't wade through a website that doesn't easily and quickly take them to where they want to go.

CONTACT AND SOCIAL MEDIA ABOVE THE FOLD

If you have ever had to search a site for a company's contact information or social media connections, you know how irritating it can be. Branding

Color Me Blue, or Maybe Red

"This is a popular color right now."

"I like the color blue."

"Our logo has red in it, so let's go with that."

These are some of the typical reasons I hear as to why a particular color(s) is chosen for a website. No consideration is given to the psychological impact those colors have and how that impact lines up (or doesn't) with the brand of the business. In other words, brand should drive design—not the other way around.

For example, I had one client, the CEO of an Inc. 5000 company and an expert in business growth, who needed a personal brand website. In working with his webfolks to design the site, we were looking through a whole slew of shades to determine which color palette would best represent the seven core elements of the brand, which we had previously defined. In the end we picked the following:

- Purple because it conveys high-end exclusivity

- Blue, known to generate a feeling of respectability and solidity

- Gray-green because green is the color of growth

I vetoed yellow, because yellow evokes cheerfulness, and that was out of line with my client's CEO brand. Personally, he is a cheerful person, but that's not the quality we wanted to lead with. Yellow, while it looked nice, would have given the wrong psychological message.

For more information on the specifics of which color conveys what meaning, check out my article on QuickBooks called "How Your Online Brand Can Benefit From Color Psychology" (http://quickbooks.intuit.com/r/marketing/how-your-online-brand-can-benefit-from-color-psychology).

best practice is to place your contact information and social media buttons (LinkedIn, Facebook, Twitter, Instagram, etc.) above the fold (toward the top of the page), so they can be seen as soon as someone lands on your site without scrolling down.

CALLS TO ACTION

One of the main functions of your website is to encourage visitors to engage and interact with your company. Go beyond the passive "contact us" and "friend me on Facebook" to offer people an active and immediate call to action with such offers as:

- Sign up for a newsletter
- Take a quiz
- Download an audio or video file
- Fill out a poll or survey
- Make a comment
- Pose a question
- Sign up for a webinar or teleclass
- Download an ebook or white paper
- Make an appointment for a complimentary consultation

One important benefit of a call to action is that it captures contact information and helps you build a list of potential customers and interested individuals—at least those who want to be captured. Some marketers call this an ethical bribe: "I'll give you something for free (ebook, webinar, audio file, etc.), and in exchange you give me your email address and permission to periodically contact you with information and offers."

SEARCH ENGINE OPTIMIZATION

One undeniable foundation of a marketing-oriented website is the strategic use of keywords and phrases your audience searches for in order to optimize your website for search engines. Because sites such as Google are always altering their algorithms, SEO remains a controversial and ever-changing field. You may want to consult with an expert to help you decide what the balance should be between your paid and organic search, the best strategies for your "on-page" SEO (factors on your website), a plan for your "off-page" SEO (link building, social media, bookmarking, etc.), and which keywords and phrases offer you the greatest opportunity for top ranking.

RESPONSIVE DESIGN

We live in a world of screens—big and small. According to the Pew Research Center, 64 percent of American adults now own a smartphone of some kind, and one in five conduct most of their online browsing on their mobile phones.

"Day by day, the number of devices, platforms, and browsers that need to work with your site grows," wrote Jeffrey Veen, design partner

---

Yes, Professional Writing Matters

This is so basic I'm almost embarrassed to bring it up, but more than half the websites I audit for new clients don't make the grade. The words on your website need to be clear, concise, and accurate when describing your business and brand. If you're lucky enough to be a good writer (good, not just okay), then by all means create your own content. For most of the clients I deal with, however, writing is not within their wheelhouse, so hiring a professional is the smart move.

However, just because someone is a professional writer (or claims to be), that does not make them the right person to pen your website. They don't need to be an expert in your field, but they do have to resonate with who you are and what you do. They need to be able to capture your voice and write in a tone that reflects your brand. To find this magical scribe, ask clients and colleagues for references, look online for people who have experience writing for your industry, and read at least a few of the things they have written before committing to a contract.

---

at True Ventures in San Francisco, California. "Responsive web design represents a fundamental shift in how we'll build websites for the decade to come."

That, as it turns out, is an understatement. In one survey from Google (reported on by Margin Media), 67 percent of users reported they were more likely to make a purchase from a site that is mobile-friendly, and 52 percent said they would be less likely to engage with a business if the mobile experience was not up to par.

In the mobile era, designing a well-branded website means making sure your pages also work well and look great on a tablet, smartphone, and any other platforms that may come to pass.

Create Brand Consistency on Social Media

The third action in Phase One platform development is to create brand consistency on social media. So often I work with people whose social media at best has no consistency in look, tone, or content, and at worst is giving conflicting brand messages.

As a starting point, your branded website should serve as the hub of your social media world, and all other sites should take their cue from it. The same logo, colors, design elements, keywords, messages, and brand voice should transfer over. I recommend using the same or a similar profile pic and a version of the same bio across all social media platforms.

PHASE TWO: BRAND AND BUZZ BUILDING—BRAND EXPANSION AND ACCELERATION

With your platform solidly in place, you're ready to take on some serious buzz building. There are hundreds of significant tactics you can use to build brand and buzz, but unless you're a Fortune 500 company, you likely won't have the time or money to pursue them all. Most of the small businesses, entrepreneurs, and CEOs I encounter find that choosing three to five core strategic elements is both manageable and sufficient. The most common categories of tactics include:

- Traditional public relations (PR)
- Publishing/content marketing

- Social media
- Speaking (including podcasting, webcasting, conferences, and radio)
- Networking
- Awards/honors

The trick is to sit down and carefully consider which of these tactics (based on your business, brand, personal preferences, time, money, and energy) you are going to include in your overall brand- and buzz-building strategy.

Too often people with a high FOMO (fear of missing out) quotient are afraid to exclude a tactic. "But everyone says we have to be on Facebook," goes the refrain. In my experience, a "throw it at the wall and see what sticks" approach doesn't work. I'd much rather see my clients pick just two tactics they can do wholeheartedly and well than six they implement poorly.

In Chapter 3 you will dig deep into your brand map and be guided through a process to determine which tactics—and in which combination—will produce the best outcome for your brand. Since social media is a crucial element for most companies today, Chapter 5 offers a site-by-site guide on how to sync up all your social media with the brand map you will have just created in Chapter 3.

PHASE THREE: THOUGHT/INDUSTRY LEADERSHIP—BRAND AUTHORITY

You have carefully articulated your brand, built a stellar website, and created a ton of buzz. Your brand is steadily gaining ground, and the time has come to break out and become the "it" girl, guy, or company in your field. In other words, you are ready to make the leap into thought leadership (for individuals) or industry leadership (for companies). Either way, making that leap generally requires the following.

Adding Something New

While thought and industry leaders have an in-depth knowledge of their area of expertise, they don't rest on their laurels. They are not just reporting on what's happening in their field—they are adding something new through academic research, clinical research, experimentation, field study, and sometimes just old-fashioned, deep, reflective thinking.

Being a Trusted Source of Information

As I said at the top of this chapter, you are a thought/industry leader when the world says so. Thought leaders are a trusted source of information. Being a requested speaker at industry conferences, a go-to source for media interviews, and a contributor to blogs, leading websites, and publications are all indications that you are poised for thought/industry leadership.

Consistently Generating High-Quality Content

Thought/industry leaders generate high-quality content consistently. They create traditionally published books, ebooks, blogs, articles, podcasts, webinars, online products, and more.

I don't know anyone who has achieved thought/industry leadership without having a major content-marketing strategy in place that shows his or her value, knowledge, expertise, and leadership.

WHERE ARE YOU ON THE MARKETING MASTERY PYRAMID? TAKE THE QUIZ

I think it would be remiss of me to point out the pathway and then not give you a chance to see where you are on it. Figure 2.2 is a simple ten-question quiz that will help you easily determine what phase of the Marketing Mastery Pyramid you are in. You can also take this quiz for free on my website at www.karenleland.com.

Now that you have an idea about where you currently stand on the Marketing Mastery Pyramid, you're ready to create a strategy to take your brand to the next level. Start by taking a fresh look at how you articulate your brand by going through the Brand Mapping Process© in the next chapter.

The Marketing Mastery Pyramid Quiz

Consider each question below, and assign it a rating from 1 to 5 based on the following scale:

- 5 for regularly and consistently
- 4 for frequently
- 3 for once in a while
- 2 for rarely
- 1 for not at all

Go with the first answer that occurs to you. Don't overthink or rationalize it. The feeling you get in your gut is usually the right one. In addition, don't base your answer on where you hope to be someday in the future, but on where you are today. When you are finished, add all your points together to get your total score.

1. We use social media such as LinkedIn, Twitter, Facebook, Pinterest, or other platforms to build brand awareness, engagement, and traffic to our website. _____

2. We are proactively engaged in media outreach about our business to both online and offline outlets such as blogs, radio, magazines, newspapers, and television. _____

3. We can clearly articulate our brand messages and speak authentically and easily about our brand attributes, promise, and uniqueness in less than two minutes. _____

4. We speak at industry conferences, association meetings, and other groups that would be interested in our business and/or area of expertise. _____

Figure 2.2: The Marketing Mastery Pyramid Quiz

The Marketing Mastery Pyramid Quiz, continued

5. We have identified the most important keywords for our business and integrate SEO into our website copy, blog posts, articles, and other content. _____

6. We have developed substantial quality content such as blog posts, articles, ebooks, white papers, podcasts, or videos around our area of expertise and used these for lead-generation and lead-nurturing purposes. _____

7. We have defined the profile and characteristics of our ideal client and have developed marketing materials, services, and free offers that speak to his audience. _____

8. We update our website as needed so that it is well-designed, well-written, and on brand. In addition, our website incorporates best practices such as social media, calls to action, and offers designed to create engagement. _____

9. We have written a substantial ebook or full-length book (self-published or traditionally published) and spend time and energy promoting it. _____

10. We have a specific personal or business brand strategy in place, regularly monitor it, track the results, and adjust as needed. _____

Total Score _____

10–17 Points. Platform Development

You've taken some of the actions needed to design your brand online and off and create a solid foundation for growing your brand. To move to the next level—and before you begin any significant social media marketing or buzz building—you'll want to do three things:

Figure 2.2: The Marketing Mastery Pyramid Quiz, continued

The Marketing Mastery Pyramid Quiz, continued

1. Ensure that you have a highly functional website that acts as a hub for all your internet marketing activities in social media.

2. Clearly articulate your brand.

3. Set up or expand your social media efforts.

18–34 Points. Brand and Buzz Building

You have a core platform in place and are taking steps to effectively market your brand and business. To take it to the next level, consider:

1. Developing a steady stream of high-quality content, be it blog posts, podcasts, white papers, or ebooks

2. Regularly distributing socially relevant and timely press releases

3. Doing ongoing blogging and blogger outreach

4. Sending out a monthly or quarterly online newsletter

35–50 Points. Thought or Industry Leadership

You have built a successful platform and implemented a solid plan for getting your brand out in the world. You can build on this momentum and take your brand even deeper into thought and industry leadership and become a go-to source by increasing your visibility. To move to the next level:

1. Make reporter outreach a priority.

2. Get to know the reporters in your industry.

3. Write a traditional book.

4. Reach out to conferences and apply to speak.

Figure 2.2: The Marketing Mastery Pyramid Quiz, continued

CHAPTER THREE

The Brand Mapping Process©

Seven Core Elements of a Powerful Business, Team, and Personal Brand

B
efore you begin this chapter, I strongly recommend you read the previous ones, as they will give you a context for the following information and make this process more powerful. If you just can't control yourself, at least read Chapter 2: The Marketing Mastery Pyramid to understand how this process fits into building and promoting your overall brand.

- How can today's CEOs, startup founders, C-Suite executives and entrepreneurs act as role models for the values and priorities they espouse while simultaneously shepherding initiatives from creation to implementation in high-demand work environments?
- What does it take for a team—be they an intact group, a special project team, or a board of directors—to align on how they want to be perceived by their various constituencies and create a strategy for bringing their brand and business to the next level?

- How can individual contributors identify their own unique and authentic way of working to achieve peak performance and enhance their career opportunities?
- What is required for a startup to find its sweet spot and speak about it clearly to potential investors, customers, and employees?
- How can an established small business gain a competitive advantage and grow through reputation and referrals in a global marketplace?

One important element in all these is branding. Your brand, whether personal, team, or business, is not just a single statement or a clever quip but a multilayered, congruent narrative told across multiple channels—both online and off. The power is in knowing how to tell the story.

There are as many models for how to create a brand and tell its story as there are recipes for guacamole on the internet. While the ingredients of a strong brand are essentially the same (think avocados, onions, tomatoes, etc., just to continue the metaphor), the way they are discovered, put together, and articulated varies.

For more than a decade, I have guided hundreds of clients, their teams, and their companies through the Brand Mapping Process©. Small businesses, entrepreneurs, Fortune 500 executives, startup founders, boards of directors, and cross-functional, leadership, and intact teams have used this process to develop their authentic brands by design, rather than by default.

This process is meant to help you craft a conscious brand—one that is true to your inner purpose, deepest gifts, and unique contributions. It is not a clever way to spin who you are (and what you do) just so you sound good to other people or impress them with your magnificence.

Taking the time to work your way through the questions and exercises in this chapter will help reveal the authentic assets that will bring your brand promise into reality. The following seven core elements of the Brand Mapping Process© are critical to creating your brand identity—speaking about and promoting your brand in a consistent and powerful way. In some ways your brand map is like taking a trip to the optometrist.

The last time I went, my optometrist tested me for a prescription by putting a pair of heavy glasses with multiple lenses on my face. The doctor would click a set of lenses into place and ask, "Does this make the letters on the wall look clearer or blurrier?" One way to think of these seven core elements of the Brand Mapping Process© is as individual lenses through which you can view your personal or business brand. At times there may seem to be some overlap between the various elements of your brand map. However, by plainly articulating these seven distinct lenses (that lend greater clarity to your brand) you can express your brand in a multifaceted way.

Keep in mind that when I use the word "you" in the following process, I mean whichever slice of brand you are working on. The "you" could be a CEO, an executive, a startup founder, a small-business owner, a job seeker, an intact team, or a business, and more. The seven core elements are:

1. *Anchor Statement.* What is the go-to description of who you are and what you do, sometimes referred to as an elevator pitch?.
2. *Unique Branding Proposition.* What is it about what you do, or how you do it, that makes you unique, distinct, and special? What sets you apart?
3. *Brand Tone and Temperament.* What is the consistent mood, tenor, quality, character, and manner that you bring to all your interactions?
4. *Brand Energy.* What you can be counted on to contribute—in all circumstances and at all times?
5. *Signature Story.* Why do you do what you do? What's the essential story that brought you to this place?
6. *Signature Services.* What are your core competencies and offers?
7. *Brand Enhancers and Reducers.* What are your current strengths, weaknesses, opportunities, and threats?

THE NEW YORK SKYLINE

Whenever I start the Brand Mapping Process© with a client, I use the following metaphor: If you have ever seen one of those giant puzzles of the New York skyline (the ones that take up an entire card table), you know that at the beginning, you're just looking for the low-hanging fruit—basically anything you can easily recognize.

- "There's the top of the Empire State Building."
- "Here's a piece of the Chrysler Building."
- "I think that's a corner of the 59th Street Bridge."

As you add more pieces, the image of the skyline begins to take shape, and finally when that last piece is in place, you step back and with satisfaction go "Ahhh, there it is. The New York skyline in all its glory."

The Brand Mapping Process© is similar in nature. Although the seven core elements (and the order they are presented in) may seem arbitrary, they're not. While working your way through, just concentrate on one section at a time, and don't worry about seeing the whole brand story until the end. When all the pieces of your puzzle are in place, your unique brand map will come together and reveal itself.

CORE ELEMENT 1: ANCHOR STATEMENT

Sometimes referred to as an elevator pitch, this is your brand's bottom line. I think of the Anchor Statement as the "cocktail party talk" part of your brand. If you're at a cocktail party, and someone asks, "What do you do?" your Anchor Statement is your reply. People usually fall into two categories when answering this question.

Take Your Time

When I work with my clients and their companies, the Brand Mapping Process© takes an entire day to complete. So before you jump in, I want to encourage you not to rush this process. Don't underestimate the time it can take to answer these questions and do the exercises. These seven sections require reflection, critical thinking, and often discussion. You don't need to do this all in one sitting, either. Take your time, and don't move on to another section until you have that "no stone unturned" feeling about the one you are working on.

Brand Rambling

These are the folks who can talk about their brand (personal or business) with great certainty—it just takes them an hour to do so. For example: The handsome hunk who works as a headhunter turns around and spots the sexy and smart CEO standing next to the onion dip. He approaches her, introduces himself, and after some small talk involving who knows the host of the party and how, he pops the question.

"So what do you do?" he asks.

"Well, I'm a scientist and CEO of my own biotech firm. We specialize in the mating habits of fruit flies. Their scientific name is Drosophila. Sometimes they are called vinegar flies or wine flies, but I just call them by their common name, fruit flies. At any rate, I have a particular focus on the female fruit flies' mating circuit. Many people have studied the neurons that impact the male fruit flies' mating habits, but the females have been less researched. It's exciting to study because the female fruit fly, as it turns out, is processing a lot of information in her brain in order to make a decision 'to mate or not to mate.' I'm presenting my findings at a conference in London next week. It's one of my favorite cities. Have you ever been there?"

OK, Ms. Sexy and Smart CEO, you lost the Handsome Hunk of a Headhunter (brand-wise) at Drosophila. He may still be nodding politely, but he stopped listening long ago.

Brand Confusion

Many people are so bewildered, unclear, and vague about their brand that when asked what they do, they stumble through a generic and/or muddled response that has no impact and can even leave a negative impression. For example, I was recently speaking at a conference and began a polite exchange with the woman seated next to me at the luncheon. Here's how the conversation went:

> *Me*: "Nice to meet you. What do you do?"
> *Her*: "I'm a coach."
> *Me*: "What kind of coaching do you do?"
> *Her*: "I work with women on making their dreams come true."

Me: "What kind of dreams?"

Her: "All kinds. I help women find their passion and be happier."

Me: "How do you do that?"

Her: "With my coaching program."

Me: "What specifically do you do in your coaching program?"

Her: "I help women identify what their dreams are and what they
    need to do to make them happen."

Me: "How's your chicken?"

Her: "Fine."

She lost me at "find their passion and be happier." Don't get me
wrong, I think a good coach is worth their weight in gold. And I'm
certainly in favor of women (or anyone) making their dreams come true.
As for happiness—I'm a big fan. I just could not for the life of me figure
out what this woman was bringing to the table, how she specifically
delivered it, why she was qualified to do so, and what the real value (and
result) of her work was.

Brand Clarity

The goal of the Anchor Statement is brand clarity. Consider that
the human brain is hardwired to find patterns, and our psychology is
structured to assign meanings to those patterns. In terms of branding,
when you can explain what you do in a way that the listener can quickly
and easily fit into a pattern, you have achieved brand clarity. If you can't,
they rapidly tune out.

The Nature of an Anchor Statement

While the Anchor Statement is only the tip of the branding iceberg, it
is nonetheless an important starting point for answering the question
"What do you do?" at a conference, a corporate meeting, or, yes, a
cocktail party.

One of my clients—a lawyer specializing in business issues—told me
she became so clear (and confident) in her Anchor Statement that she
closed a client while standing in line waiting to buy movie tickets. A few
things to keep in mind about the Anchor Statement:

- *The Anchor Statement is designed to be brief and to the point.* It is not the total picture of your brand; it's the one- or two-minute go-to description. To go back to my puzzle analogy, it's the Empire State Building, not the whole skyline.
- *There are layers to the Anchor Statement.* The core of the statement is a sentence or two, but additional talking points can be woven into a conversation, time and interest permitting.
- *Your Anchor Statement does not need to be sexy.* Some schools of thought advocate for a scintillating elevator pitch that immediately captures the hearts and minds of those you tell it to. While this is occasionally achieved, for example, "I'm an astronaut, and my next assignment is to go to Mars to look for signs of intelligent life," that's a bar that most people can't—and don't need to—reach.

The basic goal is to have an Anchor Statement that resonates with your audience. Here are a few examples from some of my clients.

MICHELLE SEILER-TUCKER, M&A ADVISOR

Core Anchor Statement: I specialize in selling businesses and represent more than 10,000 buyers looking to acquire a company. On average we obtain a 20 to 40 percent higher selling price than what the business first appraises for.

Here are some additional talking points:

- I love my business because I get to help owners of small businesses and entrepreneurs who are worried they are never going to be able to retire create financial freedom and come up with a plan to eventually stop working.
- We are a leading building, buying, and selling authority. The industry has a 40 percent success rate; we have a 98 percent success rate.
- I've sold 300 businesses in 15 years, and 90 percent of the businesses I obtain, I sell.

LaGRANDE FAMILY FOODS GROUP, AGRICULTURAL COMPANY

Core Anchor Statement: We innovate and respond to the needs of our ever-changing world by building on our 160-year agricultural tradition of providing superior food products and services.

Some additional talking points for this company would be:

- We are involved in the whole life cycle of rice from kernel to kitchen, including growing, storing, milling, packaging, and distributing it.
- Planet Rice is our consumer-facing brand targeted at health-conscious individuals.
- Our Valley Select brand provides ingredients such as sprouted grains to cereal and soup manufacturers.
- In addition, we provide value-added services to other agricultural food producers, including private-label grain products.

JEANINE BOULD, OWNER, FASHION KNIT

Core Anchor Statement: I own a knitting store with a focus on stitching and stillness. We teach knitting as a path to meditation and transformation.

Other talking points:

- We help our customers make beautiful things for themselves, their family, and their friends.
- Our goal is to give our customers both the excitement of starting a project and the satisfaction of finishing one.
- We create a place to connect.

Forming Your Anchor Statement

Now it's your turn. To begin to design your Anchor Statement, use the following exercise. Grab something to write with (old-fashioned or electronic), sit in a quiet place where you won't be interrupted for at least half an hour, shut your door, and power down your cell phone.

I want you to pretend that it's one year from today, and you are sitting in a booth at a restaurant. It's one of those booths that have no back, so you can't see the people behind you, but you can overhear their conversation. After a few minutes, you realize the people in the booth are a group of your clients and colleagues, and what they are talking about, to your surprise, is either:

- You (your personal brand)
- Your company (your business brand)
- Your team (your team brand)

For this exercise, choose one of the above, take a few minutes to write each answer to the following questions:

What Would You Want to Hear Them Say About What You Do?

In other words, if I followed you around with my iPhone recording you during the working day, what activities would I catch on video? What specific actions would compose your work?

Caution: The question here is what you would *want* to hear them say about what you do, not what you think they would say or what you would expect them to say. By having you make this one year from today, I'm asking you to create your desired brand future.

What Would You *Want* to Hear Them Say About the Results You Produce?

In other words, what are the outcomes, impacts, end products, and consequences you would want people to say they received by working with you or your business, reading your book, or using your product or service?

What Would You *Want* to Hear Them Say About the Qualities with Which You Do Your Work?

In other words, what are the contributions, characteristics, talents, and virtues you bring to the party?

The Be, Do, Have of Your Brand

Now step back and take a look at the answers you just wrote down for all three questions. The first answers relate to what you "do" as part of your brand. In other words, it describes the fundamental activities that define your work or business. For example:

- A dental hygienist cleans teeth and shows patients the proper way to floss.
- A business law firm writes up contracts, advises on business law, and crafts clever letters designed to get the other side to say "uncle."
- A movie producer oversees budgets and herds cats (i.e., manages directors, actors, and other talent).
- A human resource-consulting firm creates training programs, writes personnel policies, and outsources employee assistance programs.

- A CEO speaks at industry conferences, holds weekly executive staff meetings, and counsels an underperforming executive with a poor attitude.

The "Doing" part of our brands is a fairly straightforward description of the day-in, day-out behaviors that make up our work. What you do is the service that you (or your company) offer, the process you put in place, or the product you provide. It's the way most people talk about their brands.

This isn't bad, by the way. Remember what I said earlier about our brains being hardwired to find patterns? The "do" part of our brands helps satisfy this need in others. But while this part of branding is necessary to clearly communicate, it is usually the least interesting aspect. Stay with me on this . . .

Next, take a look at the answer you wrote down for question two, about the results you produce. This relates to the "having" aspect of your brand. In other words, this is what people will "have" in terms of results, impacts, and outcomes from engaging with your brand. For example:

- The dental patient will have bright, shiny teeth and a world-class flossing ability.
- The small-business owner will win her case and have an iron-clad contract.
- The cast and crew of the movie will have a smooth and professional experience making the film.
- The employee will easily be able to apply for maternity leave and will clearly understand the parameters of that leave.
- The underperforming executive will have a breakthrough in productivity and attitude.

Many people articulate their brand (business, personal, or team) in terms of what they provide to their clients and customers, defining it by the results they produce. While this is more interesting than just describing your brand as what you "do," it's still not the complete picture. Hang on; we are almost there . . .

Finally, take a look at the answer you wrote down for the third question, regarding the qualities you contribute. These relate to the "being" aspect of your brand. In other words, these are the qualitative characteristics you bring to what you do. It's the bigger picture of the results you produce. It's the *why* behind it all. For example:

- You generate well-being for your patients, since they feel confident, relaxed, and secure that their dental health is in good hands.
- You generate peace of mind for your business clients, since you help remove the stress that can be associated with legal matters.
- You generate a family feeling among the cast and crew that makes the set feel like a safe and happy place to be.
- You generate an environment where employees are satisfied, loyal to the company, more engaged, and, as a result, more productive.
- You generate a team of executives who are constantly growing in their skills, abilities, and attitudes.

In my experience, the most powerful part of our brand is the "being" part, yet ironically, that's the aspect we spend the least time articulating. What we are contributing with what we offer (do) and the results we produce (have) are important—but the biggest difference we make is with what we bring to the party by what we are (being).

For this reason it's important that the layers of your core Anchor Statement include all three levels of brand definition: what you *do*, the results you *have* your clients produce, and the way you are *being* that makes the difference (see Figure 3.1 on page 42).

If you take a moment to review the sample Anchor Statements on the preceding pages, you will see how they contain all three elements.

Now it's your turn. Take some time, and, using the answers you wrote down, take a crack at crafting the Anchor Statement for your brand.

Once you have something you feel works, try it out on people you meet at cocktail parties, conferences, and even standing in line at the movies. Keep what resonates, and tweak the rest. It won't take long before you have an Anchor Statement that sings the true tune of your brand.

MAKE YOUR ANCHOR STATEMENT CONVERSATIONAL

Remember, your Anchor Statement is not something you repeat robotically word for word, the way you would recite a poem you learned

Figure 3.1: **The Be, Do, Have Diagram**

in sixth-grade English class. It's meant to be a spoken tool with layers that get woven into the conversation. For example, using my client Michelle Seiler-Tucker, the business broker from earlier, she might have an exchange with someone she meets at a conference that would go something like this:

> *Conference attendee*: "What do you do?"
>
> *Michelle*: "I'm a business broker. I specialize in selling businesses."
>
> *Conference attendee*: "Really? What type of businesses do you sell?"
>
> *Michelle*: "All kinds. I have a list of more than 10,000 buyers who are looking to acquire a company."
>
> *Conference attendee*: "That must be hard to match up. How big does a business have to be to get sold?"
>
> *Michelle*: "There is definitely an art and science to it. I have a process I developed that helps my clients get a 20 to 40 percent higher selling price than what they first appraised for."
>
> *Conference attendee*: "Wow, that's impressive."
>
> *Michelle*: "I love my business because I like helping small-business owners and entrepreneurs, who may feel stuck, come up with a plan to create freedom and eventually retire from their businesses when they decide to stop working."

In this example, Michelle is talking about her brand from all three points of view:

1. Specialize in selling businesses (Do)
2. Clients get a 20 to 40 percent higher selling price over what their business first appraises (Have)
3. Create freedom (Be)

The goal is to have your Anchor Statement be solid enough that you can easily talk about your brand from all three points of view in a natural, conversational way.

CORE ELEMENT 2: UNIQUE BRANDING PROPOSITION

I don't believe in ruthless competition. I honestly think that if you're great at what you do (or make, or build, or offer), there is enough work to go around. I do, however, believe in positioning, specifically in articulating how your brand speaks to the needs of your audience and the unique way you address those needs. If your Anchor Statement answers the question "What do you do?" the Unique Branding Proposition (UBP) answers the question "Why you?" Some of the key specific attributes a UBP may contain include:

- Specialized background, education, training, or experience you possess
- Proprietary or detailed processes you have created and use with clients
- Specific talents that set you apart
- Content, industry, or another niche you have expertise and/or experience in
- Unique solution to a common problem that you are addressing in a new or unusual way
- Something you do or offer that is hard to imitate/replicate

Ken Courtright is the founder of Today's Growth Consultant, and a master "Growth" strategist. His UBP is that he has worked with more than 3,300 businesses, created over 200 revenue streams for his family, and has created an Inc. 5000, multi-million-dollar business with 30 employees.

Another client, Elizoebeth Jensen, consultant to creative entrepreneurs, has a UBP that centers on the fact that after almost a decade of serious management consulting, she pursued her dream and began a successful jewelry line. Experience in both the creative and business fields gives her a strong position from which to promote her consulting. Her tagline, "Putting the business in creative," mirrors her UBP.

Still another client of mine, a senior global brand strategist, in the online retail industry provides thought and industry leadership to grow the company brand and weave a cohesive strategy across functions. Her UBP is that she's worked in every aspect of a consumer-facing brand and as a result takes a system vs. silo approach to branding.

Find Your UBP

The clearer you are about your positioning (personal or business), the easier it is for potential clients and customers (who are the right match for what you offer) to see themselves working with you. To begin identifying and articulating your Unique Branding Proposition, do the following exercise.

Audience-Desired Attributes

Take out a sheet of paper (yes, a real one), and divide the page into five vertical columns. Label the first column "Attributes," and write down a list of the attributes you believe are most important to your audience. Remember that your audience is defined by the brand (CEO, personal, business, team, executive, entrepreneurial, thought leader, etc.) you are looking to promote.

What critical criteria are that particular audience using to determine whom to hire, promote, buy from, etc.? For example, in my line of work, the key attributes potential clients often screen for in a branding and marketing consultant include:

- Experience in public relations and placement of clients in media outlets online and off
- Writing skills, including blogs, books, and articles
- Knowledge of specific social media best practices for branding

- Ability to create and shape an online presence, including LinkedIn profiles
- Proven process for branding a person or business
- Specific deliverables the client can expect from an engagement
- Prior experience working with a similar type of business, industry, or situation
- Access to implementation methods of the branding and marketing activities needed, including website development, PR placements, ghostwriting, etc.
- A good fit in terms of personality, style, and ways of working

Keep in mind that depending on the client's objectives, these attributes won't be of equal importance. For instance, the author of an upcoming book is more likely to be concerned with PR experience, while the CEO looking to build a personal brand may be more focused on the social media and writing skills of the consultant.

Now it's your turn. In the first column, make a list of the main attributes your audience is looking for.

How Do You Rate?

Label the second column on your sheet "Rating," and considering each attribute individually, assign yourself a number on a scale of 1 (very poor) to 10 (superstar) for how well your current brand matches each desired attribute.

The Hot Zone and Not Zone

Next, label column three "Zone," review each attribute, and assign it a zone according to the following scale:

- *Not Zone.* If your score was a 6 or below on any of the attributes, you are in the Not Zone with this aspect of your brand, and it's likely hurting your competitive advantage. For those attributes where you are falling short, create a strategy to bring them up to par.
- *Neutral Zone.* If your score was a 7 or 8 for an attribute, you are in the Neutral Zone for this aspect of your brand, and it's currently not strong enough to be a candidate for your UBP. Ask yourself what you could do to bolster this attribute and bring it into the Hot Zone.

- *Hot Zone.* If your score was 9 or 10 for an attribute, you are in the Hot Zone for this aspect of your brand, and it's likely a part of your UBP.

HOW DO YOUR COMPETITORS RATE?

Label column four "Competition," and rate your competitors (as a whole or by specific name) on a scale of 1 to 10 for how well their current brand matches each desired attribute. How did you stack up? Take a look at each individual attribute, and compare the numerical difference between you and your competitors. Make a checkmark next to those attributes where you are falling two or more points below your competitors. These attributes are the place where your competitors may be gaining a UBP over you. At the very least, you'll want to bring your score up to par.

QUANTIFYING YOUR HOT ZONE ATTRIBUTES

Label column five "QQ" and for each one of your Hot Zone attributes, list the strong qualitative or quantitative aspects of your brand that relate to that attribute and why it matters. For example, let's take the attribute of writing ability, some of the quantitative/qualitative points for the person might include:

Hot Zone Attribute: Writing Ability

Quantity/Quality Aspect: Author of several books, former journalist for a newspaper, blogger for a popular online site, freelance writer with more than 300 articles published in magazines and newspapers, experienced ghostwriter for blogs, ebooks, book proposals, and articles for clients, which have resulted in major media placements and book acquisitions from major publishers.

Why This Matters: Many business people are great talkers, but not great writers. Our fictitious marketing person has broad experience as a journalist (online and off) which gives her a distinct and unique advantage over someone else who has insufficient writing skills, lacks experience, or subcontracts the writing out to a third party.

CRAFTING YOUR UBP STATEMENT

Finally, to prepare you to write your UBP, answer these two questions:

1. What is it your audience doesn't know that they don't know about what they want? In other words, what it is you provide that they may never have thought about or articulated, but when they hear it, a light bulb goes off and they say, "Yes; that's what I'm looking for."
2. What do you do that is difficult to imitate? What do you bring to the party that is hard for most of your competition to match?

Remember:

- Your UBP does not have to be an out-of-the-box quality. It can be something as simple as depth or breadth of experience.
- Your UBP does not make you better (or worse) than anyone else; it's just what gives your brand its particular flavor. There's a right fit for everyone.
- Your UBP can be a combination of factors, including your talents, experience, and even attitude.
- Your UBP can include any proprietary processes, systems, methods, or techniques you have created.

Armed with the answers to the two questions above, your Hot Zone attributes, and quality and quantity specifics, take a crack at articulating your UBP.

CORE ELEMENT 3: BRAND TONE AND TEMPERAMENT

My mother tells me that when my brother Scott was a baby, he would lie peacefully in his crib for hours watching the mobile my parents had hung above the bed. I, on the other hand, was so agitated at not being able to touch the darn thing that they had to take it down. I'm still that way. An essential part of my brand quality is that I love to roll up my sleeves, get my hands into the mix, and bring structure and clarity to things.

Our fundamental character, disposition, outlook, and spirit are qualities we can usually perceive all the way back in our childhood. The same is true for our personal brand tone and temperament, aka our brand personality, character, and mood. In terms of a business, we can clearly see brand personality playing out daily. Consider how Apple is known for their *friendly, innovative design,* Disneyland for their *family-oriented fun,* and Walmart for *basics at value and price.*

Understanding and articulating your brand's core personality traits (be it business, team, or personal) is critical to creating a consistent brand across all platforms and an essential first step in forming your overall brand identity. The visual elements that make up your brand identity can include:

- Overall color palette
- Logotype
- Fonts
- Logomark
- Website design and layout
- Business name
- Images
- Background and clothing choices for headshots

Failing to articulate your brand tone and temperament prior to selecting these elements can lead to brand identity choices that are inconsistent, inappropriate, and even harmful to your overall brand. Without exception, I often hear tales about how someone spent money on a logo, website, or collateral materials that in the end just didn't seem to fit. In 99 percent of the cases, the brand tone and temperament were not deeply explored as part of the design process.

On the other hand, a clear knowledge of brand personality can make choosing the elements of your brand identity a much smoother and more successful process. For example, Ericka Curls Bartling, a business attorney whose brand tone and temperament was "a critical thinker with a persuasive yet friendly negotiation style."

To translate this into a web design, we needed to strike a delicate visual balance between the harder-edged quality of "persuasion" and the softer tone of "friendly."

We ended up with an atypical lawyer's site with warmer colors; clean, Zen-like images; and single-sentence, bold branding statements. While this approach would not be the right one for every business law firm, for Curls Bartling P.C., it was an accurate reflection of her personal brand tone and temperament.

What's Your Brand Personality?

The exercise in Figure 3.2 on page 50 is designed to help you identify your major brand tone traits. To begin to define your brand personality, take a look at the lists of qualities and traits below. Narrow down these lists by picking ten words total that you feel describe you or your business most of the time, under the widest possible set of circumstances.

If you are saying, "Only ten? Don't you know I am a multifaceted, fully realized professional (or company) with a plethora of top-notch brand personality traits?" Well, yes I do, but a true brand tone and temperament is composed of a limited set of leading qualities. When choosing your top ten, look for the following:

- The quality is consistent across the board (for a personal brand, this means at work, play, and home).
- As far back as you can remember, you (or your business) have had this quality/trait.
- People often comment to you that they feel you (or your business) possess this quality.
- People describe you (or your business) to others as having this trait.
- You feel like this quality is a major part of what you (or your business) bring to the party.
- You don't have to think about expressing this quality; it just seems to be there most of the time.
- This trait is the most representative of the group of traits it is related to (e.g., friendly might be the main trait, but it includes other nested qualities such as warm, personable, people-oriented, etc.).

LIST OF BRAND QUALITIES

To make this list a bit more manageable, I've organized these traits into four general quality groups. These groupings borrow from some common categories used in assorted personality type assessments. They are:

1. *Analytical qualities.* These reflect our logical, methodical, rational, orderly, and systematic abilities.

What's Your Brand Personality?

Analytical Qualities

_____ calm

_____ conservative

_____ dependable

_____ detailed

_____ disciplined

_____ efficient

_____ fair

_____ methodical

_____ observant

_____ organized

_____ practical

_____ precise

_____ punctual

_____ rational

_____ realistic

_____ reliable

_____ responsible

_____ thorough

Achiever Qualities

_____ ambitious

_____ articulate

_____ assertive

_____ autonomous

_____ candid

_____ confident

_____ decisive

_____ dedicated

_____ determined

_____ driven

_____ entrepreneurial

_____ independent

_____ industrious

_____ persistent

_____ productive

_____ structured

_____ tenacious

Agreeable Qualities

_____ adaptable

_____ appreciative

_____ approachable

_____ authentic

_____ collaborative

_____ compassionate

_____ congenial

_____ conscientious

_____ considerate

_____ cooperative

Figure 3.2: What's Your Brand Personality?

What's Your Brand Personality?, continued

_____ empathetic	_____ curious
_____ flexible	_____ dynamic
_____ friendly	_____ eager
_____ generous	_____ energetic
_____ helpful	_____ enthusiastic
_____ inclusive	_____ imaginative
_____ pleasant	_____ influential
_____ poised	_____ innovative
_____ polite	_____ inquisitive
_____ personable	_____ intuitive
_____ sincere	_____ optimistic
_____ tactful	_____ outgoing
_____ thoughtful	_____ passionate

Animated Qualities

_____ adventurous

_____ cheerful

_____ creative

_____ persuasive

_____ resourceful

_____ spontaneous

_____ visionary

Now take your top-ten list and prioritize it from 1 to 10, with 1 being the quality that is most like you (or your business) and 10 being the one that is least like you. What are your top three qualities? Take a few minutes and look up the synonyms for each of your top three. Do they seem to fit? By sorting this list down to those few essential qualities that you feel best represent the personality of your brand, you position yourself to create a brand identity that is in powerful alignment with your overall brand tone and temperament.

Figure 3.2: **What's Your Brand Personality?,** continued

2. *Achiever qualities.* These reflect our go-getter, self-starter, accomplishment, drive to succeed, and desire to prosper abilities.

3. *Agreeable qualities.* These reflect our amiable, good-natured, people-oriented, cooperative, and compassionate abilities.

4. *Animated qualities.* These reflect our expressive, animated, enthusiastic, vibrant, and creative abilities.

One note: Almost everyone possesses at least some qualities from each of these four groups. However, you may notice that your qualities tend to cluster in one or two areas. Remember, the point of this exercise is to begin to hone in on your (or your business's) essential brand tone and temperament.

CORE ELEMENT 4: BRAND ENERGY

One of the first questions I ask every new client is, "What's the weather that you bring with you?" In other words, what are the one or two things you (or your team or business) can be counted on to contribute? If the brand tone and temperament is the mood of your brand, your brand energy is the élan—the flair, aptitude, and talents you bring—always and under almost any circumstance. Over the past 20 years, I've observed 12 archetypal brand energies that most personal and business brands fall into. They are:

1. Advocate
2. Maker
3. Connector
4. Motivator
5. Synthesizer
6. Fixer
7. Implementer
8. Visionary
9. Interpreter
10. Storyteller
11. Facilitator
12. Mentor

While theoretically, we all have equal access to any of these energies, we usually move naturally into developing one or two of them to their fullest potential—either through circumstance or inclination.

Know Your Brand Energy Limitations

By knowing your limitations, you can ask for help when you need it. I've seen countless startup founders who were brilliant conceptualizers—full of energy at the idea stage, but petered out when it came to implementation (that is, growing the business beyond their capacity to manage it). That's largely because they had too much ego to say "That's not in my wheelhouse" and get a team around them who could make up for their skill gap—instead of being yes-men (and women).

Knowing what your particular brand energy is helps you craft your brand-building strategy. By understanding your natural strengths, you can align your brand to fit who you authentically are as an individual, team, or business.

One note: I've described the following archetypes from an individual point of view, and I've given an individual example for each type, drawn from clients and friends. However, keep in mind that teams and businesses can also embody these brand archetypes.

I strongly suggest reading through all 12 of these archetypes before determining which one or two brand energies you feel fit your brand best.

Advocate

People with this brand energy are known for their strong, unwavering support of causes and policies they believe in. No matter the situation, they're always a spokesperson for their campaign—but not in an annoying way. Individuals with a true brand energy of advocacy inspire others with their dedication. The types of statements they might make about themselves include:

- I am fully committed to this cause. It's my life purpose.
- I'm willing to stand up for what I believe, even if it upsets some people.
- I believe that eventually the work I contribute to this cause will create change.

For example: Lynne Twist, author of *The Soul of Money* and cofounder of the Pachamama Alliance, has worked with everyone from Mother

Teresa to the Dalai Lama on issues such as alleviating poverty and hunger to supporting social justice and environmental sustainability. There's never a time when I've been with Lynne—from a board meeting to a dinner party—where she's not speaking about her passionate causes. Other words that describe this energy are *activist*, *campaigner*, and *champion*.

Maker

People with this brand energy are masters at hands-on action. From cooks to software developers, they bring things physically and mentally into being. They create something that did not exist before they applied their imagination, intelligence, and skill. The types of statements they might make about themselves include:

- I enjoy spending time alone creating things.
- I get excited when I have made something myself.
- I love learning new techniques I can use creatively.

For example: Anna Zoitas founder and CEO of Seven Deuce Inc., a specialty food product company, merges the homegrown food culture of her grandparents in Greece with her family's retail food experience in New York. This has inspired her to create quality foods, crafted in small batches. Among them fine olive oil, coffee, jams, and spices. Other words that describe this energy are *artisan*, *creator*, and *inventor*.

Connector

People with this brand energy are masterful at bringing things together—people, projects, causes. They intuitively seem to know who or what would make a good fit. The types of statements they might make about themselves include:

- When I talk to someone, other people they should know are always popping into my mind.
- I have an intuitive sense of who would work well together and mutually benefit from connecting.
- I get a deep sense of satisfaction from putting people together with projects they could contribute to.

For example: Nicholas Zaldastani is one of those people who seems to know everyone. A graduate of Harvard Business School and serial entrepreneur, Nick is also a board member of the Duke Pratt School of Engineering. I've never been in a conversation with Nick, or seen him in a conversation, where the words "you should talk to so and so, I'll introduce you," were not uttered. You can almost see the wheels of his brain turning, thinking about whom he should connect with whom. Other words that describe this energy are *networker*, *arranger*, and *coordinator*.

Motivator

People with this brand energy have the ability to move other people to action. They're good at inspiring others to grow, collaborate, create, and participate. The types of statements they might make about themselves include:

- I enjoy inspiring others to be their best and reach their goals.
- I'm good at getting groups of people excited about a project.
- Other people tell me I have made a difference in their life and inspired them in some way.

For example: Adam Markel, the CEO of New Peaks (formerly Peak Potentials) travels all over the world speaking to audiences about personal and professional reinvention. He shares the top strategies and tools he has garnered after inspiring more than 100,000 on finding their big "why" for living. Other words that describe this energy are *cheerleader*, *influencer*, and *persuader*.

Synthesizer

People with this brand energy have the ability to bring together various elements (ideas, products, thoughts, etc.) and combine them in a way that creates something new or improved. The types of statements they might make about themselves include:

- I enjoy projects where I take multiple parts and put them together to make a new whole.

- I'm often asked to figure out how to make several separate things work together.
- People tell me I'm good at blending and combining things together to make something better.

For example: Susan Harrow is a media coach with a talent for taking information from various sources and turning it into a cohesive message that packs twice as much punch, from helping her clients figure out how to arrange their talking points into powerful sound bites for interviews, to creating white papers that sum up and simplify a tough PR topic. Other words that describe this energy are *integrator*, *blender*, and *producer*.

Fixer

People with this brand energy see problems as opportunities waiting for a creative solution. Rather than avoid problems, they embrace them as a fun challenge to overcome. The types of statements they might make about themselves include:

- I've never met a problem I couldn't eventually solve.
- I firmly believe there's always a solution to any problem.
- My motto is if at first you don't succeed, try, try again.

For example: My friend Joanne's father made his living by investing in and managing retail rental properties. She told me that every day he would go into work, put both hands on his desk, lean in, and cheerfully say, "Well, let's see what problems we have waiting for us today." Other words that describe this energy are *healer*, *restorer*, and *mender*.

Implementer

People with this brand energy seem to almost effortlessly turn goals and projects into action. They are skilled at taking an idea and making it tangible. The types of statements they might make about themselves include:

- I'm good at getting things done.
- I find it fun to make things happen.

- If I'm given a job to do, even if I don't exactly know how to do it, I'll find a way.

For example: Dana Aftab fits this archetype to a "T." I've traveled with Anne Christine, Dana, and their family, and it's one of the few times I get to sit back and just enjoy the journey. Why? Because Dana being the implementer that he is, has taken into account everyone's input and then lovingly planned every detail out in advance. Oh, and in his day job Dana is EVP of business operations for a Bay Area biotech firm—a perfect position for someone with implementer energy. Other words that describe this energy are *achiever*, *administrator*, and *executor*.

Visionary

People with this brand energy have the ability to imagine possibilities and then translate them into ideas others can take action on. They excel at thinking outside the box and are motivated by the energy of ideas. The types of statements they might make about themselves include:

- I am constantly on the lookout for something new to learn.
- I am always getting new ideas from books, movies, and discussions with friends.
- I'm good at coming up with breakthrough solutions to old problems and creating new possibilities.

For example: Binta Niambi Brown was named one of *Fortune* magazine's *40 Under Forty* and served as a Senior Fellow at the Harvard Kennedy School Center for Business and Government. After seven years as a partner in a prestigious New York law firm, Binta left and is now the CEO and founder of Fermata Entertainment Ltd. and Big Mouth Records—a startup that is innovating a new business model for the music industry.

Other words that describe this energy are *conceptualizer*, *idealist*, and *dreamer*.

Interpreter

People with this brand energy take something someone else has created and add value to it through a new translation. We have all heard a common song we know by heart performed in a totally new way and felt like we were hearing it for the first time. The types of statements they might make about themselves include:

- I can take any raw material and make it better by what I bring to it.
- I regularly build on others' ideas and make them my own by adding my twists to them.
- I'm continually thinking of ways that the things I see and use can be improved.

For example: A former film producer and a writer, Kim Bromley has an uncanny ability to take the words someone else has written, add her own interpretation, and transform them into something new. Her reputation in the theater community is not just for excellence but for taking things to the next level. Other words that describe this energy are *translator*, *transformer*, and *changer*.

Storyteller

People with this brand energy use their ability to create a powerful narrative to generate change and action in others. Storytellers usually express their brand energy through writing and speaking, and sometimes through visual mediums. The types of statements they might make about themselves include:

- I often speak in similes and metaphors to get my point across.
- I actually know the difference between a simile and a metaphor.
- I believe that one picture is worth a thousand words.
- I'm frequently told that my stories inspire and motivate people.

For example: Earlier in the book I mentioned Dewitt Jones, former National Geographic photographer and keynote speaker. Dewitt's popular presentations are a combination of inspiring stories, dramatic photographs, and simple, yet thought provoking ideas. At times he has even included live hula dancing and poetry in his keynotes, all of which he uses to weave together a cohesive narrative and paint a vivid picture for his audience. Other words that describe this energy are *narrator*, *orator*, and *minstrel*.

Facilitator

People with this brand energy have an innate talent for getting a group of individuals to engage in effective dialogue and constructive debate and ultimately come to consensus. The types of statements they might make about themselves include:

- I'm good at helping people with different points of view get aligned.
- People often ask me to facilitate meetings and even conversations between two people.
- I'm able to see all sides to a situation and help others find common ground.

For example: Colleen Rudio is famously known by her clients for the plastic box of Post-it® notes she carries around with her. Post-it® notes, which she uses to capture different ideas and points of view of the group she is working with. Never rattled by bad behavior, fragmented group factions, or a situation that looks unresolvable, Colleen takes it all in stride, knowing she can get almost any group to a cohesive decision. Other words that describe this energy are *moderator, mediator*, and *conciliator*.

Mentor

People with this brand energy often act as trusted advisors. They easily gain other people's confidence through their belief in and support of others. The types of statements they might make about themselves include:

- I often have an intuitive sense of what other people are feeling and need.
- People frequently seek out my counsel and keep me in their confidence.
- I enjoy helping other people overcome their challenges and reach their goals.

For example: My client Aaron Young is the creator of The Unshackled Owner program for entrepreneurs looking to build a business that's bigger than they are. He is one of the most ethical, generous, and kind people I know. He also went to federal prison for 14 months for an IRS matter. I won't go into the whole story (you can read that in Aaron's book). But Aaron's experiences led him to a place where he wanted to give back. His life experiences have also given him a deep compassion he brings to the students, business people, and colleagues who seek out his advice on both personal and professional matters.

Other words that describe this energy are *advisor*, *teacher*, and *guide*.

What's Your Brand Energy?

Now that you've had a chance to look through these 12 brand energy archetypes, which ones resonate with you? Again, while you may be good at many of these, there are usually a few that really stand out. Ask yourself which one or two . . .

- Am I most known for?
- Do I feel I have a natural gift or talent for?
- Do others frequently acknowledge me for?
- Do I believe I bring to almost any situation I'm a part of?
- Can I be counted on to contribute?

CORE ELEMENT 5: SIGNATURE STORY

Years ago I worked with a woman who was a vice president of finance for a high-tech series C startup in Silicon Valley. We were updating her bio in preparation for an upcoming speech. When I asked why she didn't want to use her current bio, she said, "The problem with my old bio is that it highlights the fact that I used to be a chiropractor. I don't want to say that."

"Why not?" I asked.

"It just seems weird that I used to be a chiropractor, and now I'm a VP of finance."

"Tell me what you used to do as a chiropractor," I said.

As she described her work as a chiropractor, it occurred to me that there was a parallel between her previous and current vocations.

"So let me see if I understand this," I said. "As a chiropractor, you examined the system of the body and brought what was not working optimally into alignment. As a VP of finance, you examine the financial system of your company and ensure that it's working optimally in alignment. Would that be fair to say?"

"Yes," she replied.

"So it's a different system, but a similar skill set. Did you learn anything as a chiropractor that has helped you in your current job as a VP of finance?"

"Absolutely," she replied, and explained how.

From my perspective, this connection was an integral part of her Signature Story; it also made her a much more interesting and engaging person. I recommended that she not only include her previous occupation in her bio but also integrate into her speech the parallels between being a chiropractor and a VP of finance.

As with all the other core elements of the Brand Mapping Process©, the Signature Story applies equally to your personal, team, or business brand—and there will be times when the primary means through which you share about your brand will be your Signature Story. It answers the question "How did you get here?" And, anecdotally, it highlights your contribution and competencies. Some of the qualities of an effective Signature Story include the following.

Authenticity

A Signature Story that is based on exaggeration (or even worse, lies) is neither effective nor ethical. However, a narrative rooted in reality has the power of authenticity behind it. No matter how boring or insignificant you think yours might be, there is always a grain of greatness to be found in every legitimate Signature Story.

Serendipity

We have all heard some version of this story from a newly married couple . . .

"If I had not been on that business trip to London, bent down to pick up an umbrella, pulled out my back, gone to the hospital for an X-ray, and ran into her in the hospital cafeteria, we would never have met. It was meant to be."

Everyone enjoys hearing how at some level, things unfold in the perfect way and at the perfect time. A well-told Signature Story illustrates how your personal or business brand in part came into being through fate, fortune, coincidence, or grace.

Specifics

In writing, we have a saying: "Show, don't tell." A Signature Story gives you the opportunity to highlight specific aspects of your brand through example, rather than declaration.

A Moment of Truth in Cambodia

Here's just one section of the Signature Story from Elizabeth Sheehan, founder and president of Care 2 Communities (C2C):

> At 32, on the edge of a minefield in Cambodia, my world broke open. I was there training aid workers when a distraught local grandmother pulled me toward a tiny hut. Inside, in near darkness, I could feel the heat from the wall and smell the fear and blood. I could hardly make out the frail woman who had just delivered a tiny infant. As she lay still on the dirt floor, I noticed the sarong underneath her body growing darker. She was bleeding to death—from postpartum hemorrhage. The number-one killer of women after birth, it's preventable—but deadly if not treated.
>
> I watched as her small children clung to each other in the shadows and knew their fate was as tragic as hers. Motherless children fare poorly; the mother, their soul, the glue, was fading away. I had nothing she needed—not a clinic, medicine, or blood. I stood by helpless, tears mixed with sweat pouring down my face as she passed away before my eyes.

Elizabeth goes on to explain that this was the moment that forever cemented her commitment to developing innovative and sustainable models that change the way health care is delivered in the developing world. Today, her nonprofit organization, Care 2 Communities (www.care2communities.org), offers high-quality, affordable health care through clinics that begin to sustain themselves in just a few years. In the past five years alone, they have cared for more than 42,000 patients.

The Five Core Signature Story Types

Almost every movie made or book written has at its core a distinct story type. These plotlines are the timeless way we tell tales and make our stories universal. Based on author Christopher Booker's *The Seven Basic Plots*, here are five of the most common story archetypes that can be found in a personal, business, or team Signature Story:

1. *Rags to Riches: Cinderella.* These are stories in which the hero/heroine takes a risk and it pays off. They use their gumption and smarts to put themselves in providence's way, and luck (or a fairy godmother) helps them out.

2. *Beat the Bad: Star Wars.* These are stories in which good overcomes evil; the hero/heroine beats the odds and becomes stronger, wiser, and more successful through adversity.

3. *There and Back Again: The Wizard of Oz.* The hero/heroine sets out on a journey from home. Along the road they make new friends and are often helped by an unseen (sometimes magical-seeming) force. They finally return home, wiser and more mature.

4. *Eyes on the Prize: The Lord of the Rings.* The hero/heroine goes out in search of a specific reward or accomplishment—be it the hand of the fair maiden or the possession of a treasured prize. The quest usually requires them to transform some key aspect of their psyche for success.

5. *Awakening: A Christmas Carol.* The hero/heroine begins this story as a flawed figure with a limited worldview. Over the course of the tale, they see the error of their ways (usually through the influence of a third party) and change for the better.

Bear in mind that your Signature Story might actually involve several of these key plotlines, possibly with tragic and comic moments intertwined.

Writing Your Signature Story

Now it's your turn. You will need at least 20 minutes for this exercise. Sit in a quiet place, and make some notes about the following for either you or your business:

- History of your significant past jobs, clients, and/or projects. This can include game-changing assignments that propelled you to a whole new level in your business or off on a different path altogether. What have you learned from these that you use today?
- Experiences you have had that shape who you are and what you do today. These experiences won't necessarily all be positive. In fact, some of the most powerful Signature Stories center on seemingly negative experiences that ultimately contained a great gift.
- People you have encountered along the way who have influenced who you have become. This can include mentors, company founders, family, friends, authors, clients, teachers, or random strangers on the subway.
- Talents, skills, and abilities you have gained through your unique history. These are the tangible by-products of the life/career you have experienced so far.

Now go through your notes, and shape them into a narrative that tells your story chronologically. Remember, this is not a laundry list of your accomplishments but rather the story of the significant people, places, and things that have shaped your personal or business brand.

CORE ELEMENT 6: SIGNATURE SERVICES

Remember the coach whose answer to the question "What do you do?" was "I help women find their passion and be happier"? That is not a Signature Service.

Signature Services are specific know-how, competencies, and/or offers that you, your team, or your business bring to your audience. They can include, but are not limited to, any intellectual capital (e.g., proprietary processes, unique models, specific systems, etc.) you create and name. Below are a few client examples from a diverse group of industries, both personal and business.

- *Care 2 Communities* (C2C) turns converted shipping containers into health-care clinics in the developing world.
- *Income Store*, a two-time Inc. 5000 designee, helps individuals, companies, and private equity firms buy revenue-generating websites at two times earnings.
- *Donny Epstein*, founder of the Epstein Institute, travels the world along with his wife, Jackie, treating titans of government and industry (including self-help superstar Tony Robbins) with his proprietary methods of healing. Donny is the creator of EPI Energetics and the developer of Network Spinal Analysis and the Reorganizational Healing and Living program.

Executives Have Signature Services, Too

A Signature Service is not just the purview of entrepreneurs and organizations. Executives also have Signature Services, in the particular skill set or talents they bring to their organization. For example:

- "I help individuals and teams who are experiencing confusion, inertia, or lack of movement get to the heart of the matter quickly and find meaning through dialogue and actionable feedback."
  —Leslie, VP of HR at a Fortune 500 financial institution
- "Managing complex, multicultural, and multigeographic worldwide transformation projects."
  —Nancy, chief innovation officer at a Fortune 500 high-tech company
- "Planting seeds for the future in daily conversations and combining the ability to get people on the bus with the vision for where we are going."
  —Stan, VP of marketing at a leading internet company

Clarifying what your Signature Services are as an executive allows you to make stronger choices about where to spend your time, prioritize projects, and surround yourself with others whose Signature Services complement your own.

- *The California Rangeland Trust* is a nonprofit organization founded by a group of innovative cattlemen and cattlewomen in 1998 to conserve the open space, natural habitat, and stewardship provided by California's ranches.
- *Jeanne Bliss* is founder and president of CustomerBliss and co-founder of The Customer Experience Professionals Association. Based on her extensive experience as a customer service executive in five Fortune 500 companies, she has created The Five Competencies: a proven framework to build your customer-driven growth engine.

Defining Your Signature Services

Just by reading the examples above, you may already have a clear idea of what your personal, team, or business Signature Services are. If not, make an inventory list of all the competencies you possess and services you offer. Then take each one, and see if you can articulate it more specifically, narrowly, or uniquely as a Signature Service.

If you're still stuck, try talking to a few of your clients and co-workers and asking them to add to your inventory list. They will often get to the heart of the issue immediately. Sometimes the hardest thing to see is what's right in front of us.

CORE ELEMENT 7: BRAND ENHANCERS AND REDUCERS

The final step in the Brand Mapping Process© is to examine where you stand today in terms of your current brand effectiveness (personal, team, or business). What are you doing that is enhancing your brand, and what is reducing it?

I find that a modified version of the traditional SWOT (strength, weakness, opportunity, and threat) analysis works well as a framework to uncover this information.

- *Brand Strength*: A good or beneficial quality or attribute that supports the brand
- *Brand Weakness*: A quality or feature that is disadvantageous to the brand
- *Brand Opportunity*: A circumstance that makes something possible for the brand

- *Brand Threat*: Something likely to cause damage or danger to the brand

All the information you have articulated so far in the Brand Mapping Process© will be useful in creating your brand's SWOT analysis.

Your Brand's SWOT

Consider each of the criteria below individually and, depending on your answers, assign it an S for strength, W for weakness, O for opportunity, or T for threat. Make notes about the specifics of each criterion. In some cases a quality will fall into multiple categories. In other words, one aspect may be considered a strength, while another dimension could be construed as an opportunity. In general, however, most of the criteria on the list will fall into one of the four categories.

- The brand's current competencies
- The brand's competitive advantages
- The specific experience and knowledge the brand possesses
- The brand's innovative or unique qualities or offers
- The important resources (financial, human, etc.) the brand possesses
- The critical skills the brand brings
- The brand's geographical advantage
- The education or accreditation the brand possesses
- The values, philosophy, and culture the brand represents
- The brand's price, value, or quality advantage
- Effective systems and processes the brand has in place
- The marketing and distribution capabilities the brand possesses
- The brand's delivery capability
- The way the brand is expressed and articulated

Having identified where you stand with these main brand elements, the next step is to come up with a plan to improve the strong aspects and address the weaker points. For example:

- *Strengths*. Shore up you brand's strengths by determining how you can move them to the next level. Just think, if you are always making your own brand strength's obsolete before your competitors do, you will always be ahead of the pack.

- *Weaknesses.* Identify some simple steps you can take to mend the cracks in your brand. Often these weaknesses exist as an outgrowth of brand elements never fully developed and require only a tweak or slight alteration to get back on track.
- *Opportunities.* These are the places where a little effort can go along way. Taking advantage of opportunities doesn't seem to have the same sense of urgency as resolving the threats you face. For this reason it's a good idea to actually schedule a specific time to work on making these opportunities a reality.
- *Threats.* This is the category that requires immediate attention. The threats in your brand can widen into huge cracks overnight when the market shifts, a new competitor arrives on the scene, or you begin losing business. Fixing the threats your brand faces usually requires significantly more time and effort than just addressing weaknesses. Don't let the amount of effort this may take stop you from protecting your brand and business.

Congratulations. You have done the hard work of taking a deep dive into your brand and articulating seven specific ways to craft your narrative. Now you can kick back, take off your shoes, have a glass of wine (or a martini), and wait for the business to start rolling in. Ahh, if only that were the case. Unfortunately, great branding is not an "if you build it, they will come" phenomenon.

In the next chapter you will take all of this beautiful brand information and shape it into a strategy for putting your brand—business, personal, or team—into action.

CHAPTER FOUR

The Brand Mapping Strategy

Creating Your Business and Personal Branding Plan

Your brand map, no matter how brilliantly expressed, is no more than words on paper if it's sitting in a desk drawer or even framed on a wall. Once you've defined your brand, it's time to design a strategy that communicates your brand to your audience—be they within your company, your industry, or the outside world at large. Developing an overall blueprint for your brand is a four-step process.

1. Understand the tactical landscape.
2. Determine your best tactical approach.
3. Create your implementation strategy.
4. Measure success and pivot as needed.

UNDERSTAND THE TACTICAL LANDSCAPE

I regularly meet with executives and entrepreneurs whose heads are spinning from all the possible ways they can brand themselves and their businesses. Putting together a plan begins with getting the lay of the land, so you can begin to weed out the strategies that are not a good fit and identify those that are. Here's the minimum you need to know about each of the major tactical categories to make an educated evaluation.

Traditional Public Relations

Effectively implementing this tactic usually requires hiring a professional PR or marketing firm that knows whom to contact in, and how to pitch to, the media. The tactics associated with traditional PR center on you being interviewed in the following places.

RADIO

There are three types of radio: terrestrial, internet, and satellite. Technically speaking, terrestrial radio is the traditional AM/FM type of broadcasting in which the signal is transmitted by radio waves to a receiver from an Earth-based transmitter. Internet radio, on the other hand, is broadcast over the web, wirelessly. Satellite (aka digital) radio uses direct broadcasting satellites and can usually be accessed only through paid subscription.

Many PR professionals still consider terrestrial and satellite radio interviews to be of the highest value when it comes to brand building. One reason is that the barrier to entry is significantly higher. A busy producer, who is pitched potential guests all day long, says yes only to interviewees who meet a certain level of professional achievement or expertise. In addition, the listening audiences for terrestrial radio are currently larger than most internet shows. According to the Pew Research Center, 91 percent of Americans age 12 and older had listened to traditional AM/FM radio the week before they were surveyed in 2014.

Internet radio is, however, rapidly moving into the consumer mainstream. The 2015 "Internet Radio Trends Report" from XAPPmedia estimates that the internet radio listener base will grow to 183 million by 2018, and 2015 survey data from Edison Research shows that more than

50 percent of Americans age 12 and older have listened to online radio in the past month.

Mainstream TV

Often considered the big dog of public relations, landing a spot as a guest on a national TV show (on CNN, Fox News, MSNBC, etc.) is a win for any brand. Just be aware that the competition for placement on top networks and popular shows is fierce, and more often than not it requires using the services (and paying the costs) of a PR professional.

Since virtually every national show requires video proof of a guest's TV worthiness, it's a good idea to start by getting booked on local news and morning shows in your area and working your way up.

Newspapers and Magazines

"Print is dead," say the skeptics. But mention of your business (or person) in a magazine or newspaper can be a major boon to your brand. In addition, since most hard-copy publications have an online version, the chance for live links back to your website is good. Which publications you go after placement in depends on your business, objectives, and audience. Possibilities include:

- Trade magazines are professional publications written for a defined audience, such as *Training* magazine (for HR professionals), *Plumbing & Mechanical* (for contractors), and the *ABA Journal* (for lawyers). Even though these magazines have a smaller circulation than their national counterparts, if they reach your specific customer base, they can be invaluable in building your brand.
- Popular national magazines such as *People*, *O*, *Rolling Stone*, *Men's Health*, and *Better Homes and Gardens* cater to specific audiences and demographics on a large scale. The trick is to do your research and find those that fit with your particular personal or business brand. Getting to know the editors and the freelancers who write for these publications is the road to coverage.
- National newspapers such as *USA Today*, *The New York Times*, and *The Wall Street Journal* are premium placement spots. Start by identifying columns and sections of the paper where your brand

story, news, or expertise would be of high relevance. Newspapers in particular run on—no surprise here—news. So the more current, relevant, and newsworthy the information your offer is, the better your chances of getting coverage.

Press Releases

At the heart of public relations is the timeless press release. To start, it's important to distinguish between two distinct types of press releases:

1. *Broadcast.* This involves writing a basic press release, filling out a form online, and submitting it to a press release distribution company (such as Newswire, PR Newswire, or Wired PR News). For an average cost of between $25 and $250, these services will upload your press release and send it out to a general audience, including Google News, web-sites, and reporters and writers who have opted in to the service. Note that these press releases do not go to specific editors or producers at specific shows, so the chances of spending $100 and sending out a general press release that gets picked up by *The New York Times* or the *Today* show is slim. That's not what they're designed for.

2. *Targeted.* This second type of press release is emailed to individual reporters, producers, writers, and bloggers at a list of specific media outlets. In addition, these press releases are generally written by a PR professional and are linked to an event, such as:

   - Release of new book

   - Company achievement

   - Individual achievement

   - Relevant, timely expertise

   - Award or honor

The cost of a targeted press release campaign can run anywhere from $3,500 to $30,000 a month, depending on your goals, scope, and who you hire.

- Local newspapers can offer more placement opportunities since they often put an emphasis on interviewing community members as part of their mission.

BLOGS AND ONLINE PUBLICATIONS

Top interview venues used to be the purview of big glossy magazines and top-ten newspapers. Today, top blogs (*The Huffington Post*, *Mashable*, *TechCrunch*, etc.) and online publications (Entrepreneur.com, BusinessInsider.com, etc.) carry just as much prestige. Advantages of being covered by an online site include:

- Exposure to a larger audience
- Live links back to your website
- Permanent record of the interview
- Easy access to the interview
- Keywords associated with your brand

In addition to an interview prospect, these sites often offer the opportunity for guest blogging, book excerpts, and placement of infographics.

Publishing

In my experience, one of the most effective tactics for building brand and buzz is publishing. If you or someone in your organization has top-notch writing skills, you can achieve a very high return for the time invested. Hiring a ghost or outside writer is also an option. One advantage to this strategy is that for online pieces, you can include searchable keywords and get links back to your site. Tactics in this area follow.

BLOGGING

I am totally, unabashedly, unapologetically biased toward blogging as a strategy for building a brand. It is one of the major ways I've seen brands built and people and businesses position themselves as thought leaders. Blogging as a tactic can have big payoffs. According to HubSpot:

- Companies that blog have 97 percent more inbound links and 55 percent more website visitors.

Keywords Count

I will end up using the term "keywords" dozens of times in this book. And while I don't have the space to go into all the particular ins and outs about finding and using them, there are hundreds of books out there you can consult. What I will say about keywords is that they are critical to any brand-building strategy. From press releases to blog posts, the use of keyword phrases (both short and long tail) are critical to positioning your brand in the marketplace and being found by your audience. I have consistently seen a dedicated keyword list used to organically rank on the first page of Google—without paying per click.

- B2C companies that blog generate 88 percent more leads per month than those that don't.
- B2B companies that blog generate 67 percent more leads per month than those that don't.

By the way, some people write exclusively for their own blogs, while others write primarily for other sites to establish their thought or industry leadership. Either strategy can work. The keys are quality, keyword relevance, timeliness, and consistency of posting.

WRITING A BOOK

One of the best tactics for building your personal and business brand is writing a book. However, every would-be author has a critical first decision to make. Namely, should they go with traditional publishing or self-publishing?

- Traditional publishing is where a publishing company buys the rights to an author's manuscript. In return, the author is paid an advance and negotiates royalties for future book sales. Royalties do not kick in until the advance is paid back in full. In a traditional book acquisition, the publisher edits the book, designs the cover and book layout, and handles the distribution. Publishers are usually introduced to the book through an agent, who negotiates the deal and in return gets an ongoing percentage of the author's royalties. Traditionally published books still carry more cachet. The bar for entry is higher, and there are built-in quality controls.

- Self-publishing is where an author takes a "do it yourself" approach to all aspects of the book-publishing process, including editing, cover and layout design, price, and distribution. While many authors outsource some of these functions, they are ultimately responsible for the outcomes and the costs of these services.

One of the most popular forms of self-publishing is the ebook. Most traditionally published books are converted into an electronic version that can be read on a computer or ebook reader such as a Kindle or a Nook. However, a certain percentage of self-published books are only ever made available as downloadable PDFs, including shorter ebooks, white papers, and longer-form pamphlets.

I'm a big fan of creating ebooks that can be used for establishing credibility, marketing and branding, and list building by providing the ebook in exchange for email information on a website.

Content Marketing

Content marketing is a multidisciplinary strategy that includes a plethora of tactical areas, such as blogs, podcasts, webinars, ebooks, and social media posts. Since the focus is on generating and distributing high-value, relevant content to your audience, the quality of what you put out is significantly more important than which channel(s) you decide to disseminate the information through.

Sounds easy, right? According to a 2015 report by www.CMO.com, less than 40 percent of all content marketers are effective, and 69 percent of content marketing lacks quality.

The biggest issue with self-publishing is that there is no publishing house (Simon & Schuster, HarperCollins, Penguin Random House, etc.) overseeing the process, to make sure the quality of the writing and book design are up to par. This falls on the authors, who sometimes lack the skills, discernment, and (I'm sorry to say) occasionally the concern to make certain their self-published books meet professional standards.

WRITING ARTICLES

While most blog posts average between 500 and 800 words, a full article for a magazine or newspaper runs closer to 1,500 to 3,500 words and generally involves more research and interviews with multiple sources. Having articles published in trade publications and national newspapers and magazines can add greatly to your credibility, but placing your articles can take significant effort. Editors are swamped with writers wanting to place stories, and most require a detailed query before inviting a writer to submit a piece.

NEWSLETTERS

Penning a regular email newsletter (once a month or quarter) is an effective way to stay front and center with your current audience and attract new fans. Many businesses offer a sign-up for their newsletter on their website, often in exchange for a free downloadable gift such as a podcast, webinar, ebook, or other content. Some common traits of effective newsletters include:

- They are sent out on a predictable schedule. Clients come to expect that they will receive your newsletter at given intervals, such as once a day, week, month, or quarter.
- They offer mostly high-quality content. While you may include an offer or two, newsletters that deliver value will get opened, read, and shared.
- They are branded and follow a structured template. Your newsletter should use the same visual elements as your website. In addition, by keeping the format and layout the same each time, you let readers know where to find the sections that most interest them.

Keep in mind that your email newsletter must comply with anti-spam laws, which give you permission to email only those who have opted in to receive it. In addition, be sure to put an unsubscribe link on your email so the reader can opt out at any time.

Speaking

The powerful thing about speaking as a tactic is that it puts you in front of a large audience where you are already positioned as the expert. There is nothing like talking about your topic to a room full of potential clients to elevate your credibility. While I still believe that "live" speaking has an edge over online, both are popular ways to build your brand.

PRESENTING AT CONFERENCES

This can include giving a keynote speech, offering a session breakout, or being a panelist. Regardless, presenting at a conference is the Good Housekeeping seal of approval from that organization to your personal or business brand.

CONDUCTING LIVE WORKSHOPS OR SEMINARS

If you choose to put on your own seminars, all the work to make it happen falls on your shoulders. Alternatively, associations, universities, and other networking groups often sponsor workshops for their members' benefit. The advantage is that they then do the planning, marketing, and organizing. All you have to do is show up and be brilliant.

WEBINARS AND VIDEOCASTING

One advantage of using the webinar (or videocasting) tactic is that anyone with a computer, tablet, or mobile phone (which, let's face it, is almost everyone in business) has access to your brand. In addition, with today's desktop technologies, producing a webinar is relatively inexpensive. According to a 2010 Forbes Insights report on "Video in the C-Suite," 75 percent of executives surveyed said they watch work-related videos on business-related websites at least weekly, and 65 percent have visited a vendor's website after watching a video.

PODCASTING

Have a one-hour commute? Just about to get on a six-hour flight from San Francisco to New York? Stuck waiting in a hotel lobby for your lunch date? Why not grab a pair of earphones, fire up your iPhone, and listen to a podcast?

According to a 2015 report from Libsyn, of their 2.6 billion podcast downloads in 2014, 63 percent were requested from mobile devices. In part because of its accessibility, podcasting is fast becoming a favorite tactic of brand builders everywhere. In addition, Edison Research reported in 2015 that 33 percent of all Americans 12 or older have listened to at least one podcast.

The bar for entry into podcasting is low. With an investment of a few hundred dollars, anyone can set up a virtual recording studio in their home office (or at their kitchen table) and begin broadcasting their brand message.

Networking

Despite the highly touted benefits of online connection, I still believe in the power of face-to-face networking. As someone I know once said, "Deals are made over meals." Tactics include:

- Referral marketing is a type of word-of-mouth marketing where clients and customers share about your brand with others in their network; you can also proactively ask your clients to provide an introduction to potential clients.
- In affiliate marketing, a business signs up with other companies ("affiliates") who agree to sell its products or services to their list of customers for a commission.
- Strategic alliances involve forming a partnership between two individuals or organizations who have determined that they can derive mutual value from working together. The value can be measured in terms of financial gain, increased customer reach, expanded influence, or broader knowledge.
- Networking groups, such as Young Presidents' Organization, Vestige, World Presidents' Organization, Entrepreneurs' Organization, and so on, are made up of individuals who regularly attend meetings to offer camaraderie, encouragement, and education to each other. These groups often invite guest speakers to

come in and make a presentation. Besides this one-off visitation, your personal and business brand can be greatly enhanced by being an active member.

- Research the main conferences in your industry and/or the conferences your ideal clients go to, and pick a few to attend. In addition, attending professional development workshops gives you the opportunity to spend time with like-minded individuals, who expand your network and, in turn, your brand.

Social Media

Social media is such a critical part of today's marketing and branding landscape that almost every personal or business brand must include it as part of their overall strategy.

The key is to focus on one channel (two or three at most) that caters to the audience that is best for you and then work that vertical consistently—and deeply. This can involve posting content, placing ads, active outreach, and more. There are hundreds of social media sites, but the 11 most popular are:

And the Winner Is . . .

One strategy that can add value to your brand is applying for (and receiving) an award, honor, or competitive distinction. However, since you have very little control over the outcome, I don't suggest counting on contests or competitions as a main tactic; rather, treat them as a boon that adds value to your brand.

Data-Dynamix applied for the Inc. 5000 list based on a three-year sales growth of 343 percent. They did and in 2015 were named number 1,226 on the 34th annual Inc. 5000 list. This designation gave me a newsworthy reason to create and implement a PR campaign, which landed them coverage in several top-tier media outlets.

---

1. Facebook (www.facebook.com)
2. Twitter (https://twitter.com)
3. LinkedIn (www.linkedin.com)
4. Pinterest (www.pinterest.com)
5. Google+ (https://plus.google.com)
6. Tumblr (www.tumblr.com)
7. Instagram (www.instagram.com)
8. YouTube (www.youtube.com)
9. Flickr (www.flickr.com)
10. Vine (https://vine.co)
11. Reddit (www.reddit.com)

For specific demographics and other details that can help you determine which social media sites would be your best choice, see Chapter 5.

DETERMINE YOUR BEST TACTICAL APPROACH

Now that you know the lay of the land, the trick—given your time, money, audience, talent, etc.—is to determine which of these tactics (and in what combination) will work best for building your brand.

For example, I've worked with executives and CEOs for whom writing a regular blog would've been an excellent tactic from a brand-building point of view. The only problem? They dreaded the thought.

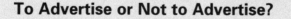

To Advertise or Not to Advertise?

That is the question. Social media has turned traditional advertising on its head. Facebook, Twitter, LinkedIn, and other outlets allow you to place ads that are narrowly targeted to a specific audience. This tactic works best as part of an overall marketing plan to generate leads, but it requires a great deal of research, setup, and follow-up to be effective.

As you can imagine, if someone hates to write, no matter how good it would be for their brand to do so, they simply won't do it. Of course, there are ways around that, including hiring a ghostwriter or recording your thoughts and having an editor turn the transcripts into blog posts and articles. However, this still requires an investment of time, money, and energy to produce.

The point is that for most entrepreneurs, executives, and small businesses, even if a particular tactic has a high return on investment, it still may not be a good choice for them. The degree to which you enjoy, appreciate, or like a tactic impacts its inclusion (or not) in your overall brand-building strategy. Bottom line: If you love a tactic, you're more likely to put in the time and effort to make it happen. Here are some of the most important factors to consider in choosing which of the above tactics you want to employ:

- Do you love it or loathe it?
- Does it offer a sufficient ROI?
- Do you have the talent, skills, or ability to pursue this tactic, or can you hire someone who does?
- Do you have the money required to pursue this tactic?
- Do you have the time required to pursue this tactic?

CREATE YOUR IMPLEMENTATION STRATEGY

Now that you have chosen the core tactics of your Brand Mapping Strategy, the next step is to determine your plan for putting them into action. For each specific tactic, consider which of the following methods you'll use for execution:

- Hire someone full time.
- Hire someone part time.
- Hire a consultant, expert, or other professional provider.
- Use an intern.
- Do it yourself.
- Delegate it to a current employee.
- Use a combination of DIY and outsourcing.

MEASURE SUCCESS AND PIVOT AS NEEDED

There are as many ways to measure the success of your Brand Mapping Strategy as there are tactics. To start you need to know what criteria you're using for evaluation. What are the primary purposes of your strategy? These can include but are not limited to:

- Attracting new prospects
- Expanding general awareness of your business/brand
- Increasing credibility and social proof of your brand
- Encouraging people to take action and buy
- Becoming more top of mind in your market
- Expanding your online presence
- Increasing your share of search
- Building a mailing list
- Generating repeat and/or longer website visits
- Converting visitors to your website
- Filling your marketing pipeline
- Attracting potential investors, partners, or affiliates
- Reaching reporters looking for experts
- Establishing thought leadership

Once you know what you want to measure, the next step is keeping your fingers on the pulse of your progress. This means periodically checking in to see what tangible outcomes are resulting from your Brand Mapping Strategy in these three general areas:

1. *Customers.* This is any result that involves closing new business, generating new leads, improving audience outreach, and increasing the flow into your marketing pipeline.
2. *Credibility.* This is any result that involves advancement in your social proof, such as positioning as a thought leader, increase in perceived authority or standing, improved online presence, and media coverage.
3. *Cash.* This is any numerically measurable financial result that brings the bucks to your bottom line—or reduces your spending.

Remember that when it comes to branding, it's a marathon, not a sprint. Don't expect that today's branding efforts will see immediate results. What you want to keep your eye on is the change over time in the number, quality, and degree of increase in customers, credibility, and cash your Brand Mapping Strategy is producing.

BEWARE THE BLOW DRYER EFFECT

Many decades ago, when I first began traveling the world for work, having a blow dryer in your hotel room was considered a luxury. In fact, you could really only expect to find one in a five-star hotel—and even then, you usually had to call ahead and request it.

Compare that to today, where every hotel room, from a Motel 6 to a Four Seasons, almost anywhere in the world, has a blow dryer in the bathroom. They have become a standard part of the hotel experience. What used to be special has become expected.

It's the same with your brand map. Something that is new, shiny, bright, and exciting today may be old, out of date, and clichéd by tomorrow. My point, of course, is that you always need to be taking a new, fresh look at your Brand Mapping Strategy based on how the world is today, not how it was yesterday. By updating your Brand Mapping Strategy as the world, market, industry, business, and customers change, you ensure that your brand (personal or business) remains relevant.

The four chapters in Part One of this book have given you the groundwork needed to design and build a basic brand positioned to take flight. To accelerate your personal, team, or business brand, read on and get ready to roll up your sleeves, dig deep, and move your brand to best of class.

PART TWO

Your Personal Brand in Action

Build

Your Brand

CHAPTER FIVE

Sync Up Your Online Presence

Positioning Strategy for Social Media

Although it's hard to imagine life without it, social media has been around for only a relatively short time. On the Small Business Trends website ("Complete History of Social Media: Then and Now"), blogger Drew Hendricks writes that the first recognizable social media site was Six Degrees, created in 1997. A mere two years later, the first blogging sites became popular—and we were off to the races.

Almost two decades later, there are hundreds of social media platforms to choose from. And if their impact on branding, marketing, and the business bottom line hasn't yet motivated you to seriously participate, you're not paying attention. Consider these findings:

- 90 percent of marketers say social media efforts have increased exposure for their business, according to a 2015 survey from Social Media Examiner.

- 89 percent of consumers use a search engine to locate what they want prior to making a purchase, per a 2012 study from Fleishman-Hillard and Harris.
- According to Erik Qualman, author of *Socialnomics: How Social Media Transforms the Way We Live and Do Business*, 78 percent of consumers trust online peer recommendations, while only 14 percent trust ads.
- 43 percent of social media users have purchased a product after sharing or favoriting it on Pinterest, Facebook, or Twitter, according to a 2013 study by Vision Critical.
- Forrester Research predicts that online shoppers in the U.S. will spend $327 billion in 2016.

As you have no doubt gleaned from the previous chapters, you can benefit greatly from using the tactic of social media in your overall brand strategy and by getting your social media in sync with your business or personal brand. This alignment starts by understanding the multitude of ways in which social media can make a difference for you.

WHY SOCIAL MEDIA REALLY MATTERS TO YOU

Despite the plethora of studies, statistics, and reports showing that an effective social media campaign has a positive impact on building a brand, many business people (including marketing professionals) remain in a foggy "I know I should be using social media, but I'm not sure how or why" state. According to one report by Social Media Examiner, 85 percent of marketers who use social media are not clear on which social media tools would work best for their business.

To see the big picture of how social media can specifically help you, consider these five impacts a social media campaign can have on your personal or business brand.

Enhanced Brand Recognition and Thought Leadership

It's simple math: The more frequently you show up on social media, the greater your brand exposure and the more recognizable (and credible) your company, personal brand, product, and business become.

For example, let's say you want to get more gigs as a speaker for your industry's top events and conferences. Today, most meeting planners start their search on Google. If you come up—not once, but dozens of times—as an expert, you're more likely to be seen as a thought leader and invited to speak. You can't buy that type of publicity. Well, actually you can, but it's expensive. It's much better to get it for free through the smart use of social media.

Increased Trust Through Leveraged Credibility

Let's say a major influencer in your industry retweets you, links to a blog post you have written, or interviews you for an article on their website. What does this say about your brand to their audience—and yours? Fundamentally it's a thumbs-up that proclaims "We have enough trust in your expertise to put our brand behind yours." That's *leveraged credibility*, and it helps create the kind of trust necessary for brand success. A 2009 study from Mext Consulting showed that if consumers trust a brand:

- 83 percent will recommend it.
- 82 percent will use its products and services frequently.
- 78 percent will look to it first for the thing they want.
- 50 percent will pay more for its products and services.

Competitive Advantage in Cold Conversions

The third social media marketing bottom line for your business or brand is a competitive advantage in converting visitors who come to you cold via internet search (as opposed to through referral or personal contact) into members of your tribe. Let's say a potential customer has narrowed the field down to you and one other competitor. If you have an active (and quality) social media presence (be it with a blog, Pinterest, LinkedIn, or another channel), and your competitor has a weak social media presence, which brand do you think is going to catch their attention? And the answer is . . . the one with the more engaging social media.

While this might not be the only criterion that will factor into their choice, we know social media does influence customers' decision making. A 2015 report on "Navigating the New Digital Divide" from Deloitte noted that customers who use social media to shop before or during a visit to a store are 29 percent more likely to make a purchase that same day. A 2011 study from the ODM Group showed that 74 percent of consumers rely on social networks to guide purchasing decisions.

Greater Percentage of Referrals Closed

A decade ago, if you were looking for a consultant in change management to facilitate your annual off-site retreat, you would call up a few of your colleagues and ask for some recommendations.

Next, with your list in hand, you would call (most likely from your land line) each of the candidates, interview them, and ask to be sent (through the mail) some marketing materials.

After perusing their various promotional pamphlets, you would narrow it down to a few finalists and call them up—or ask them to come in—for a second interview. Then you would make your decision and contract someone to do the job.

Today, if you are looking for a consultant in change management to facilitate your annual off-site retreat (which will be held live in New York with colleagues from China joining remotely), you search the keywords "change management consultant," and more than 26 million results pop up.

You can eliminate about half the results on the first few pages because you can tell at a glance that they don't match what you are looking for (job postings, Wikipedia entries, white papers, etc.) and are left with six to ten others that seem to fit the bill.

Next you click through to each potential provider and, if you're a typical user according to the Nielsen Norman Group, you spend less than a minute on each site—59 seconds, to be precise. A few consultants make the case within that time frame for why you should stay longer, by impressing you with their:

- Obvious expertise
- Social proof
- Overall credibility
- Clear brand visuals and messages
- Content that shows competency
- Easy user navigation

Having identified one to three consultants who look promising, for each of these you might look at their LinkedIn profile, check out their Twitter feed, view one of their videos on YouTube or listen to their podcast, read a couple of their blog posts or skim through an ebook, and, just for good measure, search their names. Satisfied that they are serious players in the field—and not serial killers disguised as management consultants—you fill out the contact form on their website.

You get a response back and, via TimeTrade, vCita, or other online scheduling software, you arrange a time to talk by phone. At the top of the call, they begin telling you about who they are and what they do. Politely, you stop them, saying, "There's no need to cover all that. I've already searched you and been to your website. What I need to know is this: Do you have experience facilitating these types of off-sites with some of the participants joining remotely from China?"

You repeat this process with all the finalists, make your decision, and contact your choice. They send you an electronic contract to sign, and you send them a deposit on PayPal.

The moral of this story is that the nature of referral marketing has changed dramatically, and like it or not, social media has become a factor. Even when someone you know refers a potential client to you, they are likely to begin the evaluation process online. Once you've passed that hurdle, then and only then will they feel comfortable enough to reach out and begin a dialogue.

More Cash and Customers

Finally, while social media is by no means a total solution to increasing your sales, it can't hurt. In fact, research from social sales expert Jim Keenan showed that in 2012, nearly 79 percent of salespeople who used social media in their selling process had better results than their counterparts who were not using it.

The takeaway here is that social media can act both as a flag to alert potential clients to your brand and as a funnel to flow those same people into your website, where it then becomes your job to convert them.

SOCIAL MEDIA SITE REVIEW

Most solopreneurs, small-business owners, startups, and the like don't generally have the time (or resources) to actively pursue all social media avenues. Syncing up your social media with your brand means choosing the few channels that are the best fit for your business, audience, talents, and interest level.

One note: While you may want to have a presence on a multitude of social media platforms, I suggest you choose one or two that you can commit to focusing on. The following is a brief overview of the demographics of the top four social media sites.

LinkedIn

In terms of the B2B marketplace, LinkedIn (www.linkedin.com) is the number-one player in its field. Used to build and engage with professional networks, LinkedIn sees two new members join every second. Demographic highlights include:

- 82 percent of LinkedIn users are 35 or older.
- 44 percent earn $75,000 or more per year.
- 46 percent of online adults who use LinkedIn are college graduates.
- 62 percent of B2B marketers consider LinkedIn an effective marketing tool.
- 56 percent are male.
- 44 percent are female.

Take note that much of what happens on LinkedIn is centered on the IT services, financial services, computer software, and telecommunications space. If you're a B2B provider and your audience fits this demographic, LinkedIn could be your perfect social media site.

Facebook

If the big dog in the B2B space is LinkedIn, then the king of B2C is Facebook (www.facebook.com). This is the biggest social networking site with the largest number of users. More than 1 million small or midsize businesses advertise here, and larger companies are estimated to spend as much as $100 million on Facebook advertising per year.

- 72 percent of American adults who are online use Facebook.
- That number includes 82 percent of adults ages 18 to 29, 79 percent of adults ages 30 to 49, 64 percent of adults ages 50 to 64, and 48 percent of those 65 and older.
- 58 percent of users are female.

The ten biggest industries on Facebook based on their number of fans are sports, fashion, retail food, fast-moving consumer goods, entertainment, media, electronics, auto, retail, and beauty. If you are in any of these industries, Facebook may just fit your perfect customer profile.

Twitter

Twitter (https://twitter.com) is ideal for experts with lots of content that can be broken down into 140-character chunks.

- 23 percent of all adults online use Twitter.
- 37 percent of those on Twitter are between 18 and 29 years old.
- Only 10 percent of Twitter users are 65 or older.
- 27 percent of Twitter users make an income of $75,000 or more.

If you've got a business, book, or product that rocks the house for 18- to 34-year-olds, Twitter might be a smart place for you to be.

Pinterest

Do you have a brand that translates well in pictures? If so, Pinterest (www.pinterest.com) might just be a gold mine for you.

- 30 percent of adults online use Pinterest.
- Users are on average between 25 and 54 years old.
- Women make up 80 percent of the site's users.

The most popular topics on Pinterest are home, arts and crafts, food, women's fashion, inspiration, and how-to. If your brand is highly targeted to women in the Pinterest age range and can be aesthetically translated into images, seriously consider including this site in your social media strategy.

A Few Other Key Sites

While Facebook, Twitter, LinkedIn, and Pinterest may currently be the top four social media sites, there are dozens of others in play. Here are a few relevant facts to keep in mind for each.

GOOGLE+

Google+ (https://plus.google.com) has 300 million active monthly users, 28 percent of whom are between 15 and 34 years old, and 26 percent of whom are female. The top occupations on the site are engineer, developer, software engineer, designer, teacher, and web developer. Of online adults, 22 percent visit once a month.

TUMBLR

According to their website, "Tumblr (www.tumblr.com) lets you effortlessly share anything." The 275 million blogs on the site host text posts, photos, quotations, links, music, and videos. Part of Tumblr's attraction is that its 420 million users can highly customize their sites. It's equally divided between male and female users, and 8 percent have a household income over $75,000.

INSTAGRAM

Instagram (www.instagram.com) is a popular social media site for those looking to share their stories in a purely visual way. It hosts 300 million monthly active users, 75 million of whom use the site daily. Fifty-five percent of 18- to 29-year-old internet users use Instagram, 28 percent make less than $30,000 a year, and 75 percent are from outside the U.S.

YOUTUBE

YouTube (www.youtube.com) is the second-largest search engine after Google, with 6 billion hours of video watched per month. Seventy-two percent of U.S. Millennials, 58 percent of Gen Xers, and 43 percent of baby boomers use YouTube. Electronics are the most viewed industry on YouTube.

FLICKR

Flickr (www.flickr.com) is an online photo management and sharing application that boasts 112 million users from 63 countries who have uploaded 10 billion photos—with 3.5 million more being uploaded daily. One major attraction of the site is its plethora of Creative Commons license photos, which can be used for mostly noncommercial purposes at no cost.

VINE

Vine (https://vine.co) is a short-form video blogging site featuring six-second-long videos uploaded by users. One hundred million people a month watch 1.5 billion plays (aka loops) a day, and the videos can be shared on other social media sites, including Facebook and Twitter. Almost a third of U.S. internet users ages 14 to 17 use Vine.

REDDIT

Reddit (www.reddit.com) is an online bulletin board of registered members who submit content. The uploaded content is then voted on by the community to decide its position on the site's pages, which are organized by topics such as movies, music, books, etc. It's the 14th most visited website in the United States and has 234 million unique users.

WHICH SOCIAL MEDIA SITE IS RIGHT?

The information mentioned in this chapter is just a small window into the larger story of each of the top social media sites. Here again is the list:

- LinkedIn
- Facebook
- Twitter
- Pinterest
- Google+
- Tumblr
- Instagram
- YouTube
- Flickr
- Vine
- Reddit

Which sites are right for you? Consider the following criteria in selecting, in order of importance, which social media sites would be the best for you to pursue.

Site Demographics

How do the demographics of a site match up with your ideal audience? Do the age range, gender, income level, etc., fit well with your customer profile? In short, is this a site where your audience hangs out?

Content Type and Style

The social networks you choose should fit well with the type and style of content you create. For example, if your content strategy focuses on video, YouTube or Vine would be a good choice. On the other hand, if your content is mostly pithy how-tos, Twitter would fit the bill better.

Resources Required

Every new social media site you take up has a learning curve. Do you have the time, money, talent, and other resources necessary to build your brand on the site?

Brand Fit

Once you've done your research, the final step in selecting a social media site is asking yourself how well it fits with your current brand. Going back to your brand map, do the tone and temperament, energy, and Unique Branding Proposition match the tone of the site?

SYNC UP YOUR SOCIAL MEDIA

Having chosen your main social media site(s), your first order of business is to make certain it is in brand alignment with your website in look, tone, feel, and language. This includes consistent use on all social media sites of:

- Logo
- Website colors

- Bio
- Profile photo
- Taglines
- Key brand messages
- Company and personal name

With your social media solidly in place, you're ready to jump headlong into the deep end of the personal and business branding pool. This may mean moving your career forward, taking your entrepreneurial brand to a new height, or creating a C-Suite, or parallel CEO brand, that bolsters both you and your businesses.

CHAPTER SIX

The Misguided Myths of Personal Branding

What You Need to Know That You Think You Know, But Don't, to Brand Yourself

On August 31, 1997, an article by Tom Peters simply titled "The Brand Called You" appeared in *Fast Company*. It sparked a movement that would lead to a new way of defining personal achievement—a movement that would forever change how we think about ourselves in the context of our relationship to our jobs, industries, co-workers, and even the world at large.

Whether Peters intended it or not, the idea that we as individuals are every bit as much a brand as Coke, Starbucks, or American Express was born, and it has continued to unfold—and even expand—over the past two decades.

Today, if you search "personal brand," you will be rewarded with millions of books, articles, blog posts, consultants, trainers, workshops, and more that promise to help you understand, define, and implement your personal brand. Not bad for a term that was not even in use a few decades ago. And with the invention of the internet and its focus on self-disclosure, personal branding has become a major player on the landscape of CEO effectiveness, executive leadership, entrepreneurial and startup success, and career planning. From CEO to secretary, the message is clear: If you don't define your personal brand, someone else will define it for you.

The downside of the personal brand movement is that a cluster of myths have grown up around it, which we often embrace without even knowing it. As a branding and marketing strategist, I come face to face with these myths daily. Here are a few I'd love to bust for you.

MYTH 1: PERSONAL BRANDING IS A RELATIVELY NEW PHENOMENON

While Tom Peters brought the idea of deliberately creating a personal brand into the foreground of business and career planning, it has actually been with us for hundreds of years. Think of Napoleon Bonaparte, Winston Churchill, and Charlie Chaplin—just to name a few.

MYTH 2: YOUR REPUTATION IS YOUR PERSONAL BRAND

Popular wisdom goes something like this: It's not what *you* say your personal brand is, it's what *other people* say it is. While that's true, what you're known for among your closest colleagues, friends, and family (in other words, your reputation) won't necessarily be the brand you have online—and vice versa.

MYTH 3: YOUR PERSONAL BRAND IS ALL ABOUT YOU

I am often pulled aside by executives who say in a hushed tone, "Karen, I understand the value of a personal brand, but I don't want to be seen as a braggart or an egomaniac." While a powerful personal brand can certainly be a career booster, its impact is not limited to your professional advancement. People benefit from a leader who has a positive personal brand. Research from Barna Group reported the following:

- 91 percent of employees who work for good leaders say they enjoy going to work each day.
- 80 percent say their work makes a positive difference in the world.
- 74 percent say *they* feel empowered to be a leader at work.

MYTH 4: A PERSONAL BRAND IS A GOOD THING

Not always. Have you ever worked for someone who was known for being an X@!!&? I'll leave you to fill in the blank with your favorite term of non-endearment. We tend to think of a personal brand as a halo of positive attributes that surround someone successful and respected. But some entrepreneurs, executives, CEOs, and individuals have poor reputations, which have become full-blown "bad" personal brands. Early in my career, I worked with a small bank whose president had a reputation for hurling phones at anyone who dared to deliver bad news. Did he have a strong personal brand? You bet—but it was a disruptive and destructive one.

MYTH 5: YOUR IMAGE IS YOUR PERSONAL BRAND

A well-dressed businessperson with a snappy email signature line and a ready-made elevator speech about who they are and what they stand for does not a brand make. A strong personal brand goes beyond what's seen and said on the surface to a deeply authentic expression of values, purpose, and contribution—all backed up by action. In short, a personal brand is not strategically conceived, it's authentically discovered.

MYTH 6: A PERSONAL BRAND IS NICE BUT UNNECESSARY

If your plan is to wait out this personal branding trend until it passes— think again. In reality it's been with us for centuries (see Myth 1), and whether you realize it or not, you already have a personal brand—even if it's an unwitting one. As Jeff Bezos famously said: "Your brand is what people say about you when you're not in the room." In a world where access to information on any individual is just a few clicks away, clarifying and managing your personal brand is an evergreen business skill.

MYTH 7: YOUR PERSONAL BRAND IS AT ODDS WITH YOUR BUSINESS BRAND

"I don't want to be seen as competing with my business's brand" is a refrain I hear often from CEOs and executives when I bring up the topic of crafting a strong personal brand. Done right, creating a parallel CEO or executive brand in concert with your company brand can double your business brand exposure and even be a morale booster for your staff. Think Tony Hsieh (Zappos) and the late Steve Jobs (Apple).

As Tom Peters so famously said in his *Fast Company* article, "All of us need to understand the importance of branding. We are CEOs of our own companies: Me Inc. To be in business today, our most important job is to be head marketer for the brand called You."

CHAPTER SEVEN

Defining and Refining the Three Expressions of Your Personal Brand

Building Your Personal Brand with Visual, Intellectual, and Emotional Capital

"You should come to Hawaii and take the one-week photography workshop I'm teaching in April," said my friend Dewitt Jones, a former *National Geographic* photographer and international keynote speaker.

"I don't like photography, and besides, I suck at it," I said.

"Karen, you've been an artist forever. You just don't know how to use the medium."

"Is everyone there going to be advanced amateurs and professionals or beginners like me? I don't even know how to work a camera. I'm not kidding."

"There will be a mix of beginners and more experienced photographers, but you'll be fine; I've got your back," said Dewitt.

I trusted Dewitt, loved Hawaii, and had been a painter and printmaker since I was a kid, so why not? I thought.

Fast-forward to the first night of the workshop. Ten of us are sitting out on the lanai at the Hui Ho'olana retreat center on Molokai, a rural island with no Starbucks and not one traffic light—a true taste of old Hawaii. Looking out over the tops of papaya trees toward an iconic 180-degree ocean view, we begin our getting-to-know-you session with introductions to everyone's considerable photographic experience—everyone's but mine, that is.

Within minutes my fellow photographers are deep into a lengthy discussion about f-stops that sounds something like this:

"What if you want a shot wide enough to include the whole scene but still want a narrow depth of field? Would a 24mm, f/2 work?"

Huh? The discussion goes on, and after a minute or two, I turn to Dewitt and say sotto voce, "What's an f-stop?"

The realization that I really don't know anything about photography dawning on him, Dewitt whispers back, "I'll tell you later."

I spent the next week learning from one of the world's best photographers not only the mechanics of taking pictures, but more importantly, how to "see" in a way that allowed me to create images that were an expression of my personal style and vision as an artist.

That was almost a decade ago, and today, while I'm no Ansel Adams, I've woven the joy of a new creative hobby into my life.

"What does this have to do with branding?" you may be wondering. A lot.

In the course of learning to be a photographer (and the ensuing decade of practice), I've come to see photography as a metaphor for personal branding and learned three important lessons from it.

WORK YOUR SUBJECT

A common phrase among camera clickers, this refers to exploring different angles and aspects of your subject to get an alternative view and tell a different story. Too often we get stuck talking about our personal brands from the same old vantage point.

We are our own subject when it comes to personal branding, and the more fluid we can be in how we "frame up" the different parts of ourselves, the richer a story we can tell.

THERE'S MORE THAN ONE RIGHT ANSWER

All props to Dewitt Jones for letting me use this idea, which he speaks about in his presentations. There is no such thing as the "perfect shot." If you give ten similarly skilled photographers the same camera equipment and ask them to shoot the same subject, you will get ten different photographs back. And while you might prefer one image stylistically to another, there is no one right answer as to how that photo should be taken.

The same can be said of our personal brands. There is no one right way to express our personal brands and communicate who we are. One benefit of the Brand Mapping Process© from Chapter 3 is that it allows you to articulate the seven core elements of your brand right off the bat.

A PHOTOGRAPH EXPRESSES THREE THINGS, NOT ONE

There's a purely visual element (how the image looks [color, design, style, etc.]), an intellectual element (what the photograph is saying), and an emotional element (how the viewer feels when he looks at the picture). All three of these elements are powerfully present in your personal brand and require external manifestation to shape your message. They are, if you will, the capital you possess to express your personal brand.

THE VISUAL ELEMENT OF YOUR PERSONAL BRAND

The visual aspect of your personal brand is composed of those elements that the outside world can see. They are the physical representations of your brand and include:

- Style of dress
- Color and design choices for personal branding collateral (including website)
- Headshot
- Branded background on social media
- A visual CV

Style of Dress

Do clothes really make the man—or woman? Research seems to think so. According to a 2013 paper published in the *International Journal of Linguistics* titled "Does It Matter What We Wear? A Sociolinguistic Study of Clothing and Human Values," the clothes we sport transmit a social signal. This nonverbal cue intentionally or unintentionally discloses messages that lead others to make judgments (consciously or unconsciously) about such aspects of our personal brand as:

- Degree of sophistication
- Level of success
- Economic status
- Educational background
- Credibility and trustworthiness
- Likability
- Attractiveness
- Social background and position

Steven was a senior-level manager in a large equipment-manufacturing firm. Located in one of the company's smaller regions, he was respected by his peers and seen as a creative, big-picture thinker. But despite his talents, Steven's upward corporate climb had stalled.

In a 360-degree brand audit, I discovered that Steven, while having the goods intellectually, dressed in a way that was making him seem less competent to his customers than he was. With his long hair and casual clothing style, he just didn't seem to fit the mold of an executive in his industry.

When I first brought this up, his reaction was defensive: "I'm a free-thinking rebel son of hippie parents. I don't want to give in to the shallowness of having how I dress define my effectiveness." While I understood Steven's point of view, I pressed him to understand that the physical aspect of his personal brand was impacting him—whether he thought it should or not.

I suggested he flip through men's magazines (*GQ*, *Men's Health*, *Esquire*, etc.), cut out images, and make a collage of outfits he could see himself wearing, outfits that would say "I'm a successful professional *and* a Renaissance man. I'm corporate *and* creative."

I'm happy to say that Steven was able to create a personal style that was a blend of his hard-won gravitas and gentle nature. Within a few months, he called to tell me he had been promoted to vice president of business development and was moving to Washington, DC, to begin his new job.

In fact, there is a slew of research showing the influence suitable clothing choices can have on our experience of ourselves as well as others' reactions to us. For example:

- A 2015 paper in *Social Psychology and Personality Science* showed that when subjects donned formal work attire (as opposed to casual clothing), they showed increased abstract thinking.
- One 2014 study in the *Journal of Experimental Psychology: General* asked a group of male subjects to wear their usual casual clothing, a business suit, or sweatpants. They were then asked to participate in a negotiating game with other subjects. The dressier dudes closed better deals, and the ones who were dressed down showed lower levels of testosterone.

Color and Design Choices for Personal Branding Collateral

As I mentioned briefly in Chapter 2, the role that color and design play in your personal branding collateral is undeniable. Websites, business cards, even color choices for clothing should be appropriate to your personal brand. A few things to consider in choosing your collateral color palette and overall design follow.

BRAND FIT

A 2006 study on "The Interactive Effects of Colors and Products" asserted that colors are most effective when consumers perceive them as "fitting" with a brand. Imagine the crisp, deep mint green Starbucks logo changed into a muddy brown, or the chocolaty brown M&M's logo with a vivid purple hue instead. See what I mean? Those colors just don't feel right with those brands' overall tone and energy.

AUDIENCE

Are your customers more interested in luxury or speed? Are they impulse buyers or thorough researchers? Which do they value more: making a difference or making money? The color and design direction you choose will be impacted by your audience's buying attributes, values, demographics, and even psychographic profiles.

CONTEXT

What's the environment and background your personal brand exists in? Green is often a great choice for a natural or organic personal brand (e.g., massage therapist or vegan chef). However, a different shade of green can be equally effective for a more professional services brand (e.g., accountant or business attorney).

Headshot

If you are one of those people who think you don't need a professional headshot or that the quality of your professional photo doesn't matter, think again. A 2014 study published in *Psychological Science* reported that it took less than a second for a viewer to draw conclusions about a person based on their photo. In addition, social media profiles with pictures are seven times more likely to be viewed than those without.

For such a seemingly simple task, I'm amazed at how many bad photos come across my desk daily. To make a positive impression with your headshot, keep the following in mind.

SHOW US THE REAL YOU

Avatars, cartoon characters, illustrations, or pics of a troll doll (yes, this really happened) are a poor choice for a professional headshot on your website or social media. While they might seem cute at first glance, they do not help you create a powerful visual for your personal brand. In general, a relatively current (within the past two years) photo of the real you (not a Photoshopped, wrinkle-free god or goddess) is the goal. So if you're constantly hearing "Wow, you look really different than your photo" when you show up in person, it's time for an update.

FACE FORWARD AND SMILE

According to an article in the *Journal of Psychological Science,* a profile picture where you are facing forward and smiling helps make a good first impression. In a 2014 study from the website PhotoFeeler, a smile with teeth visible increased the perception of that person's competence, likability, and influence. A laughing smile (showing too many teeth) increased likability but reduced perceived competence and influence.

HEAD AND SHOULDERS

The studies suggest that photos framed up to show head and shoulders or head to waist make the best impression. Face-only close-ups were seen as less likable, and full-body photos had a negative impact on how capable and influential the person was seen as being.

REMOVE THE DISTRACTIONS

Sunglasses, backward baseball caps, dogs (no matter how cute), surfboards, bottles of beer, weird wallpaper, and the random hands, shoulders, or arms of other people in your profile picture can all be detrimental to your personal brand. The PhotoFeeler study found that wearing sunglasses in a profile picture lowered the wearer's likability score.

DRESS YOUR BRAND

While certain studies show that more formal dress conveys greater competence and professionalism, your personal brand, industry, and audience should be the driving factor in what you choose to wear for your headshot. Are you a private banker whose clients are Silicon Valley hipster startup founders? You may want to sport a happening jacket and leading-edge designer tie. Run a private equity firm specializing in gaming and entertainment apps? A contemporary dress, not too corporate but businesslike with a fun twist, could offer the right visual brand message.

Remember, your headshot may seem simple, but it's often the first real glimpse of your personal brand someone gets—so make it a good one.

Branded Background on Social Media

Many social media sites such as LinkedIn, Twitter, and Facebook allow you to replace their generic backgrounds with customized ones featuring images and information of your choice. A well-curated and designed background can give visitors an immediate impression of your personal brand. A few elements to consider in creating your customized background include:

- Your name/company name
- Your website address
- A headshot (different from your profile pic)
- Photos of any books you have written
- A favorite quotation (by you or someone else)
- Your position or title
- Your company logo
- Colors and design elements consistent with your logo and/or website
- An important model or diagram you use in your work

Bear in mind that there are background layout restrictions for each social media site. For the best results, I recommend working with a graphics person who, for about $75 to $150, can create a customized background within the design limitations of the specific site.

A Visual CV

With the visual web all the rage, having an internet-based, multimedia resume can help you stand out from the crowd. Although it's usually limited to just one page, a number of significant design choices go into creating an effective visual CV. Your best bet is to use one of the free or low-cost services available on the web or hire a good graphic designer, who can help you translate your brand map into an effective visual message.

THE INTELLECTUAL ASPECT OF YOUR PERSONAL BRAND

For many of us, the most common way we express our personal brand is through its intellectual properties. We communicate our brands using specific language that conveys how we see ourselves, others, and our relationship to the world around us. While there are countless ways to do this, the following four actions are critical to tuning up your personal brand's intellectual expression.

1. Brand sound bites
2. Branded biography
3. Social media profiles
4. Content creation

Brand Sound Bites

How can you leverage minimal language for maximum impact?

We have all experienced that meeting or meet-up where we had less than 30 seconds to make our case. In today's limited character world, the need for an ultra-pithy presentation of our brand is essential. This "brand at a glance," if you will, functions as a cheat sheet to deliver your brand's bottom line quickly, efficiently, and with maximum impact. Take some time to review your brand map from Chapter 3 and make a one-page personal brand cheat sheet, which includes the following.

SEXY STATS AND SPECIFICS

These are the statistics and specific examples that demonstrate the competency and results of your brand. They are the proof of your personal, team, or business brand effectiveness.

TRENDS

You can show your brand's relevance to what's happening in the marketplace by showing knowledge of the leading trends in your field—and how you are at the forefront of them.

HOT TIPS AND HOW-TOS

One or two timely and helpful pieces of advice can go a long way toward establishing the credibility of your brand. The tips don't have to be world shattering, just useful.

Practice First, PR Second

"**W**hen people want to get media attention and PR, they do it bass ack-wards," says Susan Harrow, media trainer and author of *Sell Yourself Without Selling Your Soul*. "They're in a rush to send out a press release, but when the journalist or producer calls, they have an 'oh sh*t' moment because they realize they don't really know what they want to say, and they may have just blown a wonderful opportunity for media placement."

Harrow says the trick is to prepare and rehearse ahead of time. "Practice your sound bites in a role-play situation," she suggests. "Have a friend, colleague, or media trainer ask you easy, hard, and off-the-wall questions in a friendly and not-so-friendly way, and be sure to time out your answers to keep with the confines of the interview."

Harrow even recommends videotaping the role play. "The goal is to put yourself under pressure to perform before the actual interview. This way when you are doing it for real, you'll be prepared," she says. Harrow's final piece of advice? When all else fails, simply say to the interviewer, "Well, I don't know about that, but what I do know is . . ."

POINTS OF VIEW AND INFORMED INSIGHTS

Brand thought and industry leaders have strong points of view about their areas of expertise and are not shy to share them. Taking a stand for what you truly believe in—even if it's not popular or typical—can set your brand apart. In addition, being able to offer well-thought-out, fact-backed insights lends polish to the professionalism of your brand.

UNIQUE UTTERANCES AND EXPERIENCES

Have you coined any phrases, words, or slogans that are unique to your brand or have become part of the lexicon in your field? Have you developed any proprietary processes or models? The more unique you make your brand, the harder it becomes to imitate.

Branded Biography

While your profile picture, logo, or other visuals may make the first impression when a visitor lands on your website or social media, it's your biography that often inspires them to dig deeper.

Poorly written "About" sections on your website, too-short summaries on LinkedIn, and sketchy bio sections on Twitter, Facebook, and Pinterest can stop an inquiring employer or potential customer in their tracks. On the other hand, a well-written and branded biography can be a pathway to new business and expanded career opportunities.

These days, the branded biography often replaces the classic resume, since it goes beyond a boring list of your past positions and instead gives others a feel for your personal brand—backed up by your achievements and accolades. To get to a branded biography, do the following.

Show, Don't Tell

In other words, don't just make a pronouncement about how great you are—demonstrate it by providing the details that lead the reader to that conclusion themselves. For example:

- Instead of writing "I'm a creative entrepreneur," say "I've founded and sold three startups in the tech space and hold five patents."
- Instead of writing "I have a passion for building high-performance teams," say "While I was CIO of company X, my team streamlined IT to achieve a 30 percent overall reduction in technical support time."

The key to "showing" is to give specific examples of what you have done, lay out facts and figures, provide numbers, and quantify what you can do in order to tell your story.

Be Bold Without Bragging (or Lying)

While I definitely don't want to add any fuel to our already overly narcissistic culture, I do believe your bio is the one place where it pays to be bold, rather than understate your achievements.

Notice I said be bold, not lie, exaggerate, or mislead. Likewise, you don't want your bio to include the sum total of everything you have ever done. In other words, skip the debate team award you received in the sixth grade. The key is to select the specifics that speak to your audience. Here are the types of information I ask my clients to provide me with in order to tell the story of who they are in the most accurate detail possible.

- Books or articles you have written
- Speeches you have given and for what organizations
- Radio, TV, or print media interviews you have given
- Relevant degrees, awards, or honors you possess
- Relevant projects you have been involved with
- Length of time you have been in business or doing your work
- Name-recognition clients you can mention
- National or international credentials or experience you possess
- Positions you have held
- Boards you have been a member of
- Volunteer activities and charities you support
- Special relevant skills, talents, or abilities you possess

Social Media Profiles

One advantage to having a well-branded bio is that it can function as the source document for creating social media profiles that give your site visitors an immediate feel for your personal brand. I think of these profiles as a "Brand at a Glance." There are three things to consider when crafting a bio for your social media profiles.

CHARACTER COUNT

Once while reviewing LinkedIn profiles, I saw a single-sentence summary that weakly declared "Yes, I'm a freelancer who works for myself to help others with my skills."

Needless to say, this one-liner, while unarguably pithy, did not inspire me to read any further, let alone hire this person. One personal branding best practice is to take advantage of all the space provided for your social media bio on each site:

- LinkedIn has a 120-character limit for the professional headline and a 2,000-character limit for the summary.
- Twitter and Pinterest each enforce a 160-character limit for a bio.
- Instagram has a 150-character limit.
- Facebook's "About You" section allows for multiple paragraphs of information.

Once you know the prescribed limits you are dealing with, you can use one of the many free services on the web, such as Charcounter (https://charcounter.com/en), to enter your text and check your counts.

USE ALL THE BRANDING REAL ESTATE PROVIDED

Knowing the character count for each social media profile is one thing. Using the space provided to its greatest branding advantage is another that you need to take advantage of.

On LinkedIn, for example, the professional headline space (located just under your name) is prime personal-branding real estate. Too often people write only their job title and miss the opportunity to create a mini-narrative of their personal brand.

Since space restrictions don't give you enough room for full sentences, aim for the big ideas of who you are, major brand points, and keywords. Keep in mind that each social media site offers a slightly different way to take advantage of the profile space, so adapt as necessary, but maintain a consistent message across all your social media platforms.

Here are a few LinkedIn headline examples:

- Kevin Layton's headline simply read: "CEO at Data-Dynamix Inc." To better brand him and take advantage of the maximum space available, it was changed to: "CEO at Data-Dynamix Inc., Digital Marketing Strategist, Driving Revenue, Maximizing Business Value, Inc. 5000 Winner."
- Virginia Saputo's previous headline was a two-word description saying "Cheese Queen." Instead a mini-bio was crafted to read:

"Cheese Sommelier, 'What Cheese' Website, Expert World Cheeses, Inspirational Cheese & Wine Pairings, Author."

- Kate Yeager's headline featured a nondescript "Writer and Host." Post headline revision, it now reads: "Writer, Host & MC in the Tech, Travel, Food, & Entertainment Space, Lifestyle Tech, Gaming, Apps & Celebrity Interviews."

These changes, while small, elevated Kevin, Virginia, and Kate's personal brands and immediately increased the intellectual expression of those brands.

Create Multiple Versions of Your Bio

Other than the LinkedIn summary, which allows for a whopping 2,000 characters, most of your social media bios will be short. For this reason I recommend creating a Microsoft Word document with four different versions of your bio so you can cut and paste as needed.

1. *Long-Form Bio.* This is an approximately 2,000-character bio that can be used for your LinkedIn summary and any other "About" sections on websites. Keep in mind that in many cases, the long-form bio has taken the place of a CV or resume.

2. *Short-Form Bio.* This is the pithy 150- to 160-character social media bio that you will use for Twitter, Instagram, Pinterest, and many other social media sites.

3. *Conference Bio.* This is the typical 250- to 450-word (not character) bio you are often asked to provide when you will be speaking at or attending a conference.

4. *Broadcast Bio.* This is a 75- to 100-word (not character) bio that can serve as an introduction before you give a speech or media interview, or as a bio at the end of a blog post.

Remember, long or short, your goal is to create a social media bio that's bold, not boring.

In a world where 74 percent of all internet users use social media, you can count on your profiles being checked out on a regular basis. Be ready to show your personal brand best when they are.

INTEGRATE KEYWORDS

One way to express the intellectual side of your personal brand, especially on social media profiles, is to use keywords that identify your area of expertise. A 2013 report from the Indiana University School of Journalism found that of more than 1,000 reporters surveyed, more than 50 percent regularly use sites such as Twitter for researching stories. Another 2010 study from Cision reported that 65 percent of journalists use sites such as Facebook and LinkedIn for research.

Content Creation

Your branded bio, social media profiles, and brand sound bites may form the foundation for the intellectual expression of your personal brand, but the graduate-school level of cerebral connection is the *content* you create.

Content is the personal brand capital that keeps giving long after you've put it out into the world. In Chapter 4, I went over an in-depth list of the various types of content you can create as part of your strategy to build a brand. Four of the best content-creation tactics for the intellectual expression of a personal brand are:

1. Blogging
2. Podcasting
3. Videocasting
4. Authoring a book

Throughout this book, you will find more specifics on each of these tactics and how you can employ them to build your personal, team, or business brand.

THE EMOTIONAL CONNECTION TO YOUR PERSONAL BRAND

Although it's a business and not a personal brand, consider the fervent emotional connection many Apple users have to the brand. Full disclosure:

I'm one of those people. One expression of your personal brand is the emotional capital it creates. The most powerful personal brands know what they want to authentically emote and have others experience—and they are not afraid to express it. What feeling do you most want your audience to experience when they come into contact with your personal brand?

- Joy (pleasure, bliss, delight, happiness)
- Security (safety, confidence, well-being, reassurance)
- Hope (optimism, faith, anticipation, courage)
- Excitement (enthusiasm, exhilaration, eagerness, thrill)
- Glamour (sophistication, allure, prosperity, luxury)
- Effectiveness (competence, efficiency, success, ability)
- Authenticity (sincerity, honesty, genuineness, truth)
- Toughness (strength, durability, resilience, robustness)

Being clear about the emotional capital you contribute influences everything from the language you use to describe your personal brand to the colors you choose for your website and the clothing you wear.

WHEN IS IT TIME TO REBRAND?

Keep in mind that your personal brand (just like your business brand) will probably change over time and require periodic adjustments. Your decision to embark on your personal brand 2.0 (3.0, 4.0, etc.) is most often precipitated by one of the following scenarios:

- Your message has moved on, and your focus has changed. The way you used to describe who you are, what you do, or what you offer has shifted. Old language won't convey the new you.
- Your audience has moved on, and *their* focus has changed. Markets shift, trends come and go, technologies make the once brand-new and shiny old and obsolete. If your brand is speaking to an old way of working, it's time to update.
- You are pre-emptively apologizing for your brand collateral. I often meet people who, within the first few seconds of discussing their brand, say, "Oh, please don't look at my website. It's horribly out of date. It's embarrassing." Websites and other collateral materials

(including logos, colors, and fonts) that at best don't accurately reflect who you are today and at worst are a source of shame scream out for a rebrand.

- You have identified a new niche, audience, or opportunity. If the market you are going after has shifted, the way you express your visual, intellectual, and emotional capital may need to be adjusted to come into alignment with your desired audience or opportunity.

- Your audience is not responding to your offers. Even if you think your personal brand is being clearly communicated, if your desired audience just does not seem to be responding, you have an outdated, unclear, weakened, or undifferentiated brand. Regardless of the reason, you're in need of a rebrand.

- Your brand reputation has been damaged beyond repair. Whether due to your own actions or circumstances beyond your control, a brand that has been linked by association to a highly negative event or attribute may not be recoverable in its current state. For example, an entrepreneur whose consulting business bore the same name as a group that had just carried out a major terrorist attack contacted me to help her create a new nomenclature. Despite the fact that her organization clearly had nothing to do with the terrorists, the association was always going to be there in the public's mind, so that was that. A rebrand was the only way out.

- You have undergone a personal transformation. Often when an individual goes through an "eye of the needle" experience (such as a divorce, illness, or death), they find that they're simply not the same person. Newly informed by their recent ordeal, a personal brand redo is almost a rite of passage.

People who refuse to update their personal brand when appropriate and get stuck presenting themselves exactly the same way decade after decade run the risk of becoming obsolete and disconnected. Your personal brand is an organic process—not a fixed entity. Allowing room for growth, change, adjustments, and even transformations is the stuff that relevancy is made of.

PART THREE

Creating the Brand-Centric CEO and Company

CHAPTER EIGHT

Your C-Suite and CEO Brand

Creating a Parallel Brand to Drive CEO Reputation, Executive Presence, and Thought Leadership

A ll CEOs have the daily opportunity (and obligation) to build their personal brand in service of their own and their company's reputation. In addition, many companies are beginning to realize that their executives need to have polished personal brands that highlight their expertise and knowledge to an outside audience. For that reason all the recommendations in this chapter for CEO branding and reputation management can, and should, be applied to C-Suite executives.

Far from being a luxury or an exercise in ego, building an executive brand is a requirement in our digital world. According to the Burson-Marsteller "CEO Reputation Study" from 2003, 48 percent of a company's reputation can be attributed to the standing of its CEO. Like it or not, today's CEO has been pre-cast in the role of the company's chief brand ambassador. For many CEOs the key to integrating this into their role is to create a parallel brand.

RECOGNIZE THE VALUE OF A PARALLEL BRAND

A parallel brand is the perfect blend of a CEO's personal and company brands. While remaining distinct, these two brands should work in concert. In order to be maximally effective, a parallel CEO brand must:

- Complement, not conflict with, the business brand
- Be authentic and sustainable over time
- Be positive, affirming, and aspirational or intriguing, contrarian, and captivating
- Be obvious both internally to the CEO's company and externally to the public
- Simultaneously enhance the reputation of the CEO and the business

The best parallel executive and CEO brands produce a wide range of results. A 2015 study by Weber Shandwick and KRC Research reported that:

- Global executives attribute 45 percent of their company's reputation to the reputation of their CEO
- A CEO's reputation plays an important role in attracting employees to a company (according to 77 percent of respondents) as well as motivating them to stay (70 percent)
- Global executives attribute 44 percent of their company's market value to the reputation of their CEO

In addition, other benefits of a strong CEO reputation include attracting investors, generating positive media attention, and affording crisis protection.

Take a few minutes to make a list of what you believe the specific benefits of creating a parallel C-Suite or CEO brand would be for your organization at large, your employees in general, your staff in particular, your board, your investors, and, not least of all, yourself.

THE C-SUITE/CEO BRAND MATRIX

Assuming you have accepted the necessity of leveraging your personal brand for the good of your organization, the question becomes, how do

Personal/ Executive Presence	Reputation Management	Content Marketing	Thought Leadership
Are you creating your brand by design or by default?	*How are you represented online?*	*What's the best strategy to get your message across?*	*What is your flavor of thought leadership?*
☑ **Personal Brand Narrative** • 7 Key Aspects • Branded Bio	☑ **Authority Site** • Website • About Me	☑ **Keyword Identification**	☑ **PR & Media Outreach** • Radio • Newspapers • TV • Magazines • Online • Bloggers
☑ **Positioning of CEO Brand** • Messaging • Audience • S.W.O.T. Analysis	☑ **LinkedIn** • Complete Profile • Outreach Campaign	☑ **Blogging**	☑ **Awards** • Local • National • Industry • General Business
☑ **Brand Identity Collateral** • Headshots • One Sheets • Media Kit	☑ **Search Engines** • Google Alert • Photo Update • Replace Poor Content	☑ **Articles & White Papers**	☑ **Speaking** • Conferences • Keynotes • Panels • Breakout Sessions
☑ **Media Fluency** • Comfort • Competence • Sound Bites	☑ **Claim Your Name** • Personal URL on Social • Name.com	☑ **ebooks**	☑ **Publishing** • Traditional Books
☑ **Personal Gravitas** • Substance • Style • Reputation	☑ **Social Media** • Twitter • YouTube • Facebook • Instagram • Pinterest • etc.	☑ **Podcasting & Webcasting**	☑ **Outside The Company** • Causes • Boards • Philanthropy • Teaching

© *Karen Tiber Leland, Sterling Marketing Group, 2016*

Figure 8.1: **The C-Suite/ CEO Branding Matrix**

you get there? The key is to take a matrix approach in creating a strong C-Suite and CEO brand as demonstrated in Figure 8.1. This involves taking specific action in four general domains.

1. Practice C-suite/CEO reputation management.
2. Establish your thought leadership.
3. Engage in content marketing.
4. Strengthen personal and executive presence.

PRACTICE C-SUITE AND CEO REPUTATION MANAGEMENT

Any time day or night, you need only turn on CNN or check out Twitter to see how wildfire-fast information (and disinformation) can spread. As the lines between company and CEO reputation blur, and increasingly ridiculous amounts of information on individuals become readily available in just a few clicks, CEO reputation management is a mandate. To manage yours, at a minimum you need to:

- Claim your name.
- Stay on top of the search engines.
- Be a social CEO.

Claim Your Name

In the gold-rush days, would-be wealthy miners placed stakes in the ground to mark off their territory. In the digital era, CEOs and executives need to stake their claim to their name and own as much of their digital brand territory as possible. In practical terms, this means a few things.

REGISTER YOUR NAME AS A URL

Regardless of whether you are a full-time or a work-for-hire CEO or executive, registering your name for a website is essential. Even if you never create a personal brand website, you need to protect yourself from others using your name to damage your image and reputation.

While the ideal situation is to get your exact name as your URL (e.g., www.karenleland.com), with 850 million active websites on the internet, many names are already spoken for. If your name is taken, try one of the following:

- Your first initial and last name
- Your first name, middle initial, and last name
- Your first, middle, and last names
- A hyphen between your first and last name

To Dot.Com or Not to Dot.Com

There is still widespread agreement that domain names that end with .com carry the most cachet. If you simply can't find or create a .com that works with your name, consider using an alternative domain extension such as .net, .info, or .org.

- A qualifying word at the end of your name (e.g., www.janedoeceo. com)
- Try buying your name. The person who owns it may be willing to sell it for a fair price. I've even had occasions where the individual who owned a domain name was not using it and transferred it for free out of courtesy.

GET PERSONAL URL ON ALL SOCIAL MEDIA

Facebook, Twitter, Pinterest, LinkedIn, and other social media platforms allow you to generate a vanity URL that acts as a personalized domain on these sites. For example: www.facebook.com/JaneDoe, twitter.com/ JaneDoe, and www.linkedin.com/in/JaneD.

Again, whether or not you plan on ever using a social media site, the best defense is an offense, so grab your name on the main sites as soon as possible.

Stay on Top of the Search Engines

One of the first things I do when I start working with a new executive or CEO is search them on Google to see what comes up. Then I do the same on Bing and Yahoo!—the two next-largest search engine sites.

If you or one of your staff hasn't checked out what pops up when your name gets put into a search engine, your online reputation isn't being managed. Routinely googling yourself allows you to keep track of what the search engines are saying about you and take corrective actions when possible.

To stay on top of your search engine results, set a Google Alert on yourself to receive an email when you're mentioned on the web. This way you can see who is talking about you—and what they're saying. If you don't like what you see, take a proactive stance and shape the narrative of your CEO brand.

If life were fair, you would be able to remove any undesired search engine results with a single click. But, as your mother no doubt told you when you were a kid, life isn't fair. Neither, it turns out, is the internet. While it's not effortless, and certainly not perfect, there are some useful workarounds you can employ to manage how you show up on the search engines.

Replace Old Photos

One of my clients had lost a substantial amount of weight but still had old photos popping up online. She was able to contact the purveyors of these pics and request that they replace them with an updated photo. Almost all agreed, and within a short period of time, the newer photos were what came up in the search engine results.

Push Undesirable Results Down

If you want to get outdated, unfair, and inaccurate content off the first few pages of your search results, try the following:

- Write desirable new content (blog posts, articles, etc.) aimed at specific keywords to drive older, less desirable content (which features those same keywords) farther down the list.
- Create public profiles on LinkedIn, Twitter, Facebook, Pinterest, and Google+. Since these always rank toward the top in search engine results, they can push poor content off the first page.
- Use a comment and status update strategy to weigh in—using your real name, constructive opinions, and proper spelling and grammar—on forums, blog posts, articles, and social media sites.

Be a Social CEO

One key way to manage your C-Suite/CEO reputation is to participate in social media. In our continuously connected, always-wired world, customers, employees, and shareholders have a constant hunger for—and access to—information about a company and its executives. Being a social CEO is a necessity for any leader who doesn't want to get left in the online dust.

BRANDfog's 2014 "The Global Social CEO Survey" uncovered some of the primary reasons CEOs should go social or go home. According to the report, major benefits of leadership participation in social networks include better communication, improved brand image, more transparency, and improved company morale. Specifically the survey reported that:

- 75 percent of those surveyed perceive that C-Suite and executive leadership is improved by participation on social media.

- 71 percent of U.S. respondents believe that the companies of C-Suite executives and leadership teams who communicate about their core mission, brand values, and purpose on social media are more trustworthy.
- 80 percent of respondents agree that social media is now a key component of PR and communications strategy for C-Suite executives.
- 61 percent of U.S. respondents said they were more likely to purchase from a company whose values and leadership have been clearly communicated by executive leadership on social media.
- 83 percent of U.S. respondents believe that better connections with customers, employees, and investors can be built through CEO participation in social media.

In today's hyperconnected, information-driven world, CEOs and senior executives alike are expected to have an active social presence. Brand image, brand trust, and a company's long-term success depend on it.

—Ann Charles, BRANDfog Founder & CEO

Yet despite the huge upside to participation on social sites, a great percentage of corporate executives still have not jumped on the bandwagon. According to www.CEO.com's "2012 Social CEO Showdown" report, only 30 percent of Fortune 500 CEOs have a social presence on at least one network.

While there is no one right strategy for being a social CEO and C-Suite executive, as the leader in the B2B social space, LinkedIn is a must-have.

Leverage Your LinkedIn Profile

With few exceptions, almost every executive I run across has an insufficient LinkedIn profile. The with-it ones know it matters and want a profile makeover; the not-so-well-informed toss out a dismissive "No one really reads that." In fact, they do. As the premium B2B social media site, more than likely, the customers, colleagues, employees, and future employers you work with will check you out on the site.

How does this impact your CEO brand? Let's say you're scheduled to give a keynote speech at an industry conference. There's a potential investor you want to connect with, and you've found out he will be there. You look him up on LinkedIn, reach out on the site, and suggest you meet up at the conference. It's almost a certainty that he will look over your profile. Their online impression may be the deciding factor in whether he says yea or nay to your proposed meeting.

A solid LinkedIn profile makes good social media branding sense and should include:

- A current headshot
- Your current job position
- Your two most recent job positions
- Your education
- A profile summary
- Additional skills
- At least four recommendations

For a step-by-step guide on how to build your personal brand on sites including LinkedIn, Twitter, Pinterest, and Facebook, check out my online course "Personal Branding on Social Media" on www.lynda.com/Facebook-tutorials/Personal-Branding-Social-Media/417148-2.html

For Instant Access to a CEO's Brand, Consult Your Calendar

One of the hot trends right now is the release of apps that make personal branding more of a day-to-day activity. Refresh, which LinkedIn bought in 2015, integrates your calendar appointments with data from LinkedIn to give you a preview of the person with whom you have an upcoming appointment. Similar apps are being developed that will offer you a "brand at a glance" of the person you are going to meet. For this reason alone, it's critical that every executive's and CEO's LinkedIn profile be up to speed.

ESTABLISH YOUR THOUGHT LEADERSHIP

As I discussed in Chapter 2, being a thought leader doesn't happen because you declare yourself one; it happens because your audience, industry, and the world at large say you are. The process of getting there requires forethought, planning, and execution. Start by considering the following.

What Role Will Thought Leadership Play?

A big part of developing an executive or CEO brand is deciding what role thought leadership should play. Start by considering the impact a thought leadership strategy could have on you and your organization. How can your thought leadership goals align with your larger organizational goals?

Once you've made a case in your own mind, it's important to engage the support of your boss, senior management, or board of directors. Since there are always costs (PR, branding, marketing, consulting, etc.) involved in pursuing a C-Suite or CEO thought leadership strategy, it's a smart move to get buy-in before you start down the path.

What Flavor Is Your Thought Leadership?

The world of executive and CEO branding overflows with self-proclaimed experts and gurus—many of whom have not taken the time or rigorous exploration to define their thought leadership brand.

It's Impossible to See the Inside of Your Own Eyelids

I frequently talk to people who feel frustrated that they can't seem to apply what they legitimately know about branding and marketing to their own personal and business brands. When I needed to reinvent my own brand a few years ago, I was, simply put, useless to myself. I finally hired a colleague to help me rebrand. The bottom line is that no matter how competent we may be, it's hard to do this for ourselves. Or as I once heard it put, *it's impossible to see the inside of your own eyelids.*

If you have not done so already, go back to Chapter 3 and complete the Brand Mapping Process©. This will give you a base from which to extract your thought leadership positioning. In general, CEO thought leadership comes in three varieties:

1. *Celebrity.* These people are best known for their personality: Richard Branson, Tony Robbins, Oprah Winfrey.
2. *Cerebral.* These people are best known for their thinking and ideas: Bill Gates, Mark Zuckerberg, International Monetary Fund Managing Director Christine Lagarde.
3. *Consequential.* These people are best known for the results they produce: Steve Jobs, Sheryl Sandberg, German Chancellor Angela Merkel.

Where do you think you fit in? Knowing which variety of thought leadership you want to be known for affects the tactical strategy you put in place.

"The CEO Reputation Premium" report from Weber Shandwick and KRC Research asked more than 1,700 executives which external activities they felt were important for CEOs to participate in. The top eight were:

1. *Speak at industry or trade conferences.* Being invited to speak at conferences as either a keynote, breakout session, or panel participant is a solid step in creating yourself as a thought leader in your space.
2. *Be accessible to the news media.* The more reporters get to know you, the more they will call on you when they need sources to interview. In addition a proactive PR campaign can get you on the media's radar. Be it radio, television, magazines, newspapers, online outlets, or bloggers, the more known you are the stronger your thought leadership position becomes.

   One strategy for gaining media coverage is to apply for (and receive) awards. There are an endless amount of awards available on a local and national level, within your industry and the general business world at large.

3. *Be visible on the company website.* Many C-Suite executives and CEOs are in hiding when it comes to their online presence. Clear visibility on the company website, a personal website, LinkedIn, About Me profile, or other authority landing sites are needed to give people a place to discover what your brand is all about.

4. *Share new insights and trends with the public.* There are countless ways that you can share your knowledge writ large. The content marketing strategies listed in Chapter 4 and throughout this book, can provide an excellent channel for your thought leadership.

5. *Be active in the local community.* A big part of thought leadership is reaching out beyond your own business to support your local community. Local groups, causes, and philanthropic activities all contribute to your executive and personal brand. *One caution*: I advise my clients to never pick a cause solely because they think it will help them build their brand. Sticking with causes that you feel authentically passionate about will benefit your brand, but more importantly will give you a true sense of satisfaction and contribution that will be seen and felt.

6. *Be visible on the corporate video channel.* Two words here: "Media Training." Before you jump headlong into any video taping (for your corporate website or CNBC), be sure you have your sound bites down and a level of comfort and competency that represents your CEO brand.

7. *Hold positions of leadership outside the company.* In the same way that supporting local causes brings you outside the world of your own business, teaching, sitting on boards etc., helps establish your seniority in your field.

8. *Publicly take positions on issues that affect society at large.* At perhaps the highest level of thought leadership, these are the people who have transcended talking about themselves, their brand, and even their businesses to become go-to pundits for the big-picture issues impacting our world.

ENGAGE IN CONTENT MARKETING

Considering each of these eight areas above plus the plethora of tactics described in previous chapters, outline the content marketing strategy you can engage in to support and expand your thought leadership. For example: *Share new insights and trends with the public.*

Which of the following content marketing tactics—singularly or in combination—would you use to accomplish this?

- A regular CEO blog
- Writing articles
- Publishing white papers
- A weekly podcast
- An ebook
- Webcasts

The options go on. The key is to figure out which tactics would work best for you and your company, and then build your thought leadership strategy around those. Oh and don't forget, researching your keywords is critical before jumping into any content marketing strategy.

STRENGTHEN PERSONAL AND EXECUTIVE PRESENCE

Do you have it? You know, the "It" factor—that winning leadership cocktail of people skills, communication abilities, and influence over others combined with a reputation for high performance. In short—executive presence.

The question is, how can today's enterprise leaders act as role models for the values and priorities they espouse while simultaneously shepherding initiatives from creation to implementation in high-demand work environments?

I believe that personal branding is one of the key factors that influence the moment-to-moment choices that enable effective CEOs to achieve a strong executive presence. By creating a dedicated mode of living, as opposed to a default one, leaders bring their brand promise into every interaction across the board. The results are higher performance, greater influence, and increased competence, cooperation, and engagement with their staff, colleagues, customers, industry, and the public at large.

In a 2013 study from the Center for Talent Innovation (CTI), the senior executives surveyed said that "executive presence" accounted for 26 percent of what's required for promotion.

The same study showed that of the three most important aspects of executive presence—gravitas, communication skills, and appearance—gravitas by far carried the most weight and was composed of six core traits: confidence, decisiveness, integrity, emotional intelligence, vision, and reputation.

Interestingly, "The CEO Reputation Premium" report from Weber Shandwick and KRC Research revealed that similar attributes drive strong CEO reputation, including:

- Having a clear vision for the company
- Inspiring and motivating others
- Being honest and ethical
- Being a good communicator internally
- Caring that the company is a good place to work
- Having a global business outlook
- Being a good communicator externally
- Being decisive
- Being focused on customers

I think most executives and CEOs would agree that developing and refining these qualities takes a lifetime of practice. There are, however, some important ways you can use a personal branding approach to improve the odds—and speed up the process.

Assess the Current State of Your Personal Brand and Executive Presence

What do friends and colleagues say about your approach to work? Are you always invited to a certain type of brainstorming session, or are you recruited to help with particular problems? Do people enjoy working with you because you bring a creative touch, or are you able to break big issues down into bite-size pieces? Cross-reference these answers to find the similarities.

In addition to doing your own research, you may want to consider hiring a consultant to do some further assessment, including:

- Telephone interviews with selected managers, co-workers, clients, and staff on their perception of your executive presence, personal brand, and current level of advocacy.
- A confidential, 360-degree web-based questionnaire to determine the strengths and challenges of your current executive or CEO brand.
- Intake and evaluation of your current online reputation and branding collateral, including social media, bio, resume, and Google results.

Create Personal Brand Projects

Once you have a good handle on what your current personal brand and state of executive presence are, it's time to translate your personal brand

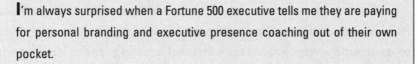

Expand the Definition of Executive Coaching

I'm always surprised when a Fortune 500 executive tells me they are paying for personal branding and executive presence coaching out of their own pocket.

When I ask why they don't just run it through HR as an executive coaching expense (which it should be), they say, "Oh, our HR department won't pay for this, since it's mostly for my personal benefit."

Really? If nothing else, I hope this book has helped you realize that any time an executive in your company improves their personal brand, they are at the same time improving the brand of your business. Their gain is your win in every measurable way possible.

into a series of targeted projects and work-specific behaviors. I encourage you to choose projects that meet the following criteria. The projects should:

- Directly benefit the individual's executive presence and personal brand, resulting in an increased leadership capability.
- Directly benefit the executive's work group, segment, or the company at large.
- Directly work toward outcomes that go beyond "feel good" to practical application on the job and/or in the leader's overall career.
- Be actionable and observable in present-day and immediate or future work-life situations.
- Be capable of completion or achieving substantial progress within a three- to four-month time frame.

Here's an example: Martha is the CIO of a large financial services firm. After discussing her personal brand and talking to some of her colleagues, boss, and staff, it became clear she was respected by the people she worked with. However, her current executive presence was not sufficient for her mandate to transform the way technology was implemented and used within the business.

In short, Martha's current brand was seen as being "a manager who effectively problem solves and is known for hands-on implementation." Not a bad brand, but insufficient for the task entrusted to her.

Martha wanted to be seen as an "influential leader who's creating a culture of continuous improvement, where people are empowered to problem solve and implement."

In light of Martha's desired executive presence, she came up with several brand projects that would begin to shift how she was perceived. One of the projects involved a series of town hall meetings designed to get her team excited about the IT transformation and buy in to supporting it. In alignment with her goal, Martha created a fun and inclusive agenda for the meeting and a highly visual presentation—the opposite of the usual boring, text-oriented presentation staff were used to.

Martha called me after the first series of town halls telling me that her meetings were the talk of the town. "Staff keep coming up to me and telling me that was the best town hall we have ever had," she said. "Their level of enthusiasm for what we are trying to do is obvious. I'm having fun."

NETWORK IN MEET SPACE

Studies show we process the communications we receive in three ways:

1. 55 percent is through body language.
2. 38 percent is from tone of voice.
3. 7 percent is through the words we hear.

The logical extrapolation is that all that emailing, texting, and writing tweets, Facebook updates, and the like leaves our audience relying on the least impactful part of communication. In the absence of body language and tone of voice, our meaning can be, and often is, misunderstood.

We have all been on both ends of that experience: the text we were offended by because we misread the tone, and the one where we unintentionally offended someone because they misunderstood ours.

It's for this reason that an executive or CEO brand that lives only in cyberspace is insufficient; the final piece of building your brand involves good old-fashioned networking in meet space. You know, the type you've practiced your whole career. So go to a conference, take someone out to lunch, pick up the phone and check in, or go attend a business workshop—your CEO brand will thank you.

CHAPTER NINE

Defining and Refining the Five Expressions of a Brand-Centric Company

Create a Culture That Gets Your Organization in Alignment with Your Brand Promise

J ust as creating a personal brand has become a key component in managing individual careers, building a brand-centric business—from startups to Fortune 500—has become a non-negotiable factor in company success. Simply having a good product is no longer enough. According to a 2012 report from Weber Shandwick and KRC Research, 87 percent of corporate executives believe that having a strong corporate brand is as important as having strong product brands.

But getting to this state of organization-wide brand focus requires creating a culture where your brand promise is woven into the fabric of how your company does business. Truly brand-centric organizations express their brand promise in five important ways that ensure a culture of alignment between the brand and the everyday way the organization behaves and functions (see Figure 9.1 on page 140).

Figure 9.1: **The Five Functions of Brand Alignment**

1. Customer experience
2. Management commitment
3. Employee engagement
4. Processes, procedures, systems, and standards
5. Organizational infrastructure

CUSTOMER EXPERIENCE

First and foremost, being a brand-centric company requires being a customer-focused one. Much has been written and said about being customer-focused over the past few decades. A Google search alone on the term brings up more than 35 million results, but fundamentally, a

> ## Staff Are Customers Too
>
> **O**ne of the hallmarks of a customer-focused company is that it has an expanded definition of the word *customer*. Instead of the more limiting meaning of the term, where a customer is someone outside the organization, the company takes a more inclusive view and considers the people who work for it as "internal customers."
>
> In fact, it usually goes one step further and has a culture in which everyone who works in the company is considered to be providing service to someone else—their customer—be they internal or external.

customer-focused company is one that pays attention to the impact its actions have on the customer experience, endeavors to proactively fulfill customer needs, and responds quickly when those needs are not met or customer expectations are not fulfilled. Being a customer-focused company requires managing three specific dimensions of the customer's experience.

The Interpersonal Dimension

This is the dimension of your customer experience that relates to the attitudes and actions your customers will encounter in dealing with your staff. The communication styles and social interactions customers have shape their experience of your brand at an interpersonal level. We have all taken an airline flight where the flight itself went as planned—it left on time, arrived on schedule, and our seat reclined properly—but the flight attendants were snarly. When this happens, our overall experience of the flight—and the airline's brand—is usually poor, despite the airline delivering us to our destination as promised.

The Product Dimension

This is the dimension of your customer experience that relates to the physical quality of the products you sell or, in the case of a service business, any tangible assets you bring to the table. Let's go back to our airline

The New Realities of Corporate Reputation

The Weber Shandwick report identified "six new realities of corporate reputation":

1. Corporate brand is as important as the product brand(s).

2. Corporate reputation provides product quality assurance.

3. Any disconnect between corporate and product reputation triggers sharp consumer reaction.

4. Products drive discussion, with reputation close behind.

5. Consumers shape reputation instantly.

6. Corporate reputation contributes to company market value.

The Weber Shandwick report concluded, "The fusion of the corporate and product reputation has only reached its tipping point today." The line between the two is becoming almost invisible.

---

analogy. If the service on the flight is friendly, but your seat's recliner function is broken and they run out of peanuts before they get to you, you are likely to have a negative impression of the carrier's brand.

One note: The product dimension of your brand experience includes your website and other marketing collateral. Since these are physical assets your customer interacts with, they impact your overall brand reputation.

The Process Dimension

This is the dimension of your customer experience that relates to how easy (or hard) it is to do business with your company. Qualities such as efficiency, speed, effectiveness, and effortlessness impact how a customer feels about your brand. An airline flight where the attendants are pleasant and you get your peanuts, but the plane leaves three hours late due to mechanical failure, will likely leave you with a bad taste in your mouth.

The bottom line is that for your company to be customer-focused, you need to align all three dimensions of a customer's experience with your brand promise. Only then will you have the foundation necessary to create a brand-centric business.

MANAGEMENT COMMITMENT

Most startup founders, entrepreneurs, and executives will readily and cheerfully tell you that a strong brand is everything to business success. The problem is that they don't always "walk what they talk" when it comes to being brand-focused. In the final analysis, it is not what leaders say about living the brand but how they actually live it that matters. The

Which Comes First, Capacity or Brand?

"**M**any businesses create a brand and then just assume their organization is going to automatically have the capacity to fulfill it," says Colleen Rudio, president of Cascadia Business Development. "I see this a lot in the non-profit sector. They put out this great big mission, but then don't have enough staff or resources to deliver."

From where Rudio sits, the issues of capacity and branding are almost never addressed in the same sentence, but they should be. "The question a business has to answer is, how are we going to systematically build toward our brand commitments with capacity, rather than promising and failing?" she says.

Rudio says the key to answering that question is to figure out what your brand-delivery non-negotiables are, match those to all the functional areas impacted, and build your capacity from there. If one of your brand-delivery non-negotiables is best-in-class service, then every decision you make has to connect with that. This means that if returning all client calls within 24 hours is a critical part of your service levels, you need to build the capacity to fulfill it, not do things the other way around by saying, "We will fulfill it when we have enough capacity [i.e., staff] to do so."

actions they take indicate to their organization (and the world at large) what is really important and valued within the company.

EMPLOYEE ENGAGEMENT

The greatest opportunity a company has to make its brand promise a reality is through engaging all its employees in the brand promise. This requires recognizing that living the brand is a job not just for the front-line staff who interact daily with customers but for everyone. From the sales department to accounting and product development to human resources, your staff are the brand ambassadors who shape your customers' (internal or external) experience.

Ironically, however, these are the people who often get the least exposure to the tenets of the brand promise and frequently get little or no training on how to fulfill their role as brand ambassadors. Brand-centric organizations recognize the critical importance of engaging their employees and providing them with the education, encouragement, and support they need to live the brand.

PROCESSES, PROCEDURES, SYSTEMS, AND STANDARDS

In many ways the alignment of your organization's processes, procedures, systems, and standards with your brand promise is the fulcrum on which creating a brand-centric company rests.

Unfortunately, too many companies ignore (at the peril of their brand's reputation) the inherent process and system problems that are negatively impacting their brand. No matter how well-intentioned, no company can achieve true brand-centricity without addressing the structural functions that work solely in the company's favor—and not in favor of the customers or employees. Being brand-centric means being willing to review and revise the ways in which your processes, procedures, systems, and standards do not line up with the brand promise.

ORGANIZATIONAL INFRASTRUCTURE

How does your company approach the people side of your business? How you define roles and responsibilities, the way you practice control and reward, the quality of recognition, and the specificity of job descriptions all have a deep impact on the brand-centric nature of your company. In order to live the brand, your business must delineate the way people in your organization work as individuals and as a team, both structurally and behaviorally.

HOW BRAND-CENTRIC IS YOUR BUSINESS?

OK, now it's your turn. The short quiz in Figure 9.2 starting on page 146 will give you an indication as to how brand-centric your company is, as well as some steps you can take to create greater alignment between your brand promise and the way your organization functions. Before you jump headlong into answering these, a few good guidelines to keep in mind include:

- If you have multiple people within your organization filling out the quiz, answer it individually before you compare your results.
- When in doubt, go with your gut feeling, and don't overthink the answers.
- Base your answers on where you are today, not where you plan on being in the future.

TWO PATHS TO BECOMING A BRAND-CENTRIC ORGANIZATION

Over the past few decades, I've seen my share of cultural change processes and company transformations attempted in organizations, including becoming more customer focused or market driven, improving employee or customer engagement, innovation, and many more. And what they all share (in common with becoming brand-centric) are the two paths organizations generally take in trying to get there.

- Path 1: The Vicious Cycle of Change Management
- Path 2: The Process of Commitment-Based Change

Path 1: The Vicious Cycle of Change Management

Too often organizations put the majority of their change-management efforts into one functional basket. In other words, rather than focus on all

How Brand-Centric Is Your Business?

Consider each question below, and assign it a rating from 1 to 5 based on the following:

5 We've nailed this

4 To a great degree

3 To a moderate degree

2 To a small degree

1 Not at all

1. Everyone in our company, regardless of their position, can speak easily and clearly about our brand attributes, promise, and distinction. _____

2. Our brand distinction and promise are clearly communicated on our website and all our other marketing collateral. _____

3. We educate all our employees in our brand distinction and promise and train them in their role as brand ambassadors. _____

4. We survey our customers to find out how satisfied they are with our brand overall and ask for their suggestions for improvement. _____

5. We survey our staff to find out how satisfied and engaged they are with the company and ask for their suggestions for improvement. _____

6. We have a process in place that allows us to make specific changes in our policies, procedures, systems, and standards to improve our brand based on customer and staff feedback. _____

7. We educate and train our managers in the skills they need (team-building, mentoring, etc.) to live the brand, including supporting staff in being brand ambassadors. _____

Figure 9.2: How Brand-Centric Is Your Business?

How Brand-Centric Is Your Business? continued

8. Our executive team meets on a regular basis to discuss the brand-centric focus of our business and the current state of our brand promise and delivery. _____

9. We regularly reward and recognize staff who excel at being brand ambassadors and deliver on the brand promise. _____

10. We have a clearly articulated brand statement that spells out our brand attributes, promise, and distinction and has been translated into long-term and short-term goals for how we run our business. _____

Total Score _____

10 to 17 Points. At the gate

You've made some strides toward becoming brand-centric, but you still have a long way to go. It's likely that your company talks a good game but in practice treats "living the brand" as a nice slogan, rather than a mandate for action. You may have even had T-shirts, mugs, or caps printed that feature the company brand commitment. Don't get stuck here for too long, or you run the risk of staff becoming skeptical and believing that "brand-centric" is just the flavor of the month. In truth, to you being brand-centric is probably a low priority compared with your financial goals and other activities that you believe have a more immediate impact on your bottom line.

The danger here is that you won't see the importance of being brand-centric until you're facing a decline in market share, loss of a major account, or other dire circumstances that force you to get your organization more in alignment with your brand promise.

18 to 34 Points. Taking off

You have the foundation of a brand-centric organization in place and are taking steps to reflect your brand in the way your company functions day

---

Figure 9.2: **How Brand-Centric Is Your Business?** continued

---

How Brand-Centric Is Your Business? continued

to day. More than likely your senior management team has bought into the idea that living the brand is good for business, but you still need to ensure that the majority of your policies, procedures, systems, and standards are in alignment with your brand promise.

Your whole company is energized by the idea of living the brand, and the attitude of "we still have a ways to go" is being met with optimism rather than skepticism. Just remember to take it one step at a time. Use a Kaizen approach (a Japanese concept meaning continuous improvement), and align your company functions with your brand promise, one fix at a time.

35 to 50 Points. Flying

Even if you have sometimes felt there was an overwhelming amount to do in becoming brand-centric, you kept charging on. With a strong foundation in place and growing momentum, you can spread your wings and innovate. However, be careful of getting stuck in the "we have arrived" mentality. Markets shift, disruptive technologies come into play, and competitors get a fire lit underneath them. Stay ahead of the curve by taking your brand to its next level.

Figure 9.2: **How Brand-Centric Is Your Business?** continued

the areas of functional alignment required to create real change, they place their bets largely on one—such as training—to drive the transformation.

Even when they do address multiple areas of functional alignment, they often implement them in an order that fails to build momentum and commitment. Instead they take a poorly planned approach, which leads to a vicious cycle where progress is slow and frustration is fast to come. Some of the most common reasons for this approach include:

- No clear understanding of what real cultural change will take
- Assigning the cultural change responsibility solely to HR
- Commitment to the appearance of change vs. real change

- Lack of alignment and participation from senior management in the change
- Lack of sufficient resources (time, money, staff) assigned to make the change happen
- Lack of structure to keep the change on track and on purpose
- Not taking advantage of external expertise available to assist with the change process

Regardless of the reason, moving forward in this way has a particular look and feel to it. By learning to recognize the various signs and stages, you can stop the vicious cycle of change management in its path and redirect. By the way, if you feel a need to run screaming from the room as you are reading the following section, skip to "Path 2: The Process of Commitment-Based Change" on page 151 and pivot ASAP. Figure 9.3 shows how it usually goes.

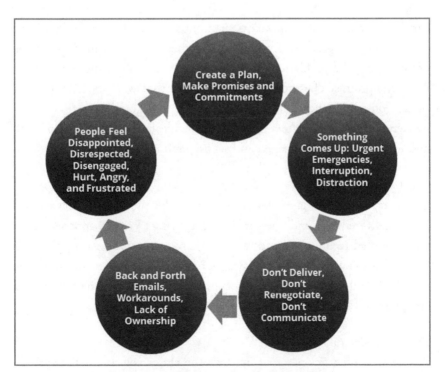

Figure 9.3: **Vicious Cycle of Change Management**

PLANS, PROMISES, AND COMMITMENTS ARE MADE

The goal of being brand-centric starts off well enough. Teams are formed at a middle management or sometimes even senior level, meetings are held, strategies created, and commitments made. Enthusiasm is middling to high, and while there may be some skepticism (or even a touch of cynicism), good intentions rule the day.

SOMETHING COMES UP

We have all heard the expression "The road to hell is paved with good intentions." At this next stage, the commitments and promises made become compromised due to distractions, interruptions, emergencies, and urgent matters that come up. This includes higher-priority items, changes in management direction, inconvenience, and dozens of other very reasonable-seeming excuses for why the plans for moving in a brand-centric direction can't be delivered on.

PEOPLE DON'T COMMUNICATE

Small or large, the commitments made and not kept have a significant impact on the process. In particular, when a commitment can't be delivered on, the problem is compounded because often the person who made the promise does not communicate that they won't be able to get it done. Sometimes they don't even attempt to renegotiate the timeline or deliverables. They just don't do it. This then leads to a whole lot of back and forth as to what happened and whose fault it is.

LACK OF OWNERSHIP ENSUES

Someone, sooner or later, figures out that the promises made are not being delivered on, and the emails start flying. What happened, who was supposed to do what, and what workarounds can be put in place? A "lack of ownership" atmosphere begins to take shape, momentum wanes, and the brand-centric cultural-change process can start to be seen as the "program of the month."

ANGER AND FRUSTRATION EMERGE

A very wise mentor once told me that the closer you are to the agreed-upon delivery time when you tell someone you can't do something you promised to do, the more upset they will be. For example, if you have a meeting with a colleague scheduled for Friday at noon, and you let them know on Monday morning of that same week that you need to reschedule, that's probably going to be fine. After all, you gave them plenty of notice.

However, if you let them know Friday at 11:45 A.M. that you can't make it, they are likely to be much more upset. If you don't tell them at all—just miss the meeting and send them an apologetic email on the following Monday—they'll really be seeing red.

That's how it goes when the promises, plans, and commitments made at the beginning of the process are not fulfilled—and not communicated. People understandably become disappointed and disengaged. They end up feeling disrespected, hurt, angry, and frustrated. It's not a pretty story, but one that must be told.

RE-PLANS, RE-PROMISES, AND RE-COMMITMENT

Even in the face of these issues, the desire to become brand-centric can live on. People pull themselves up by their bootstraps, teams are brought together once again, meetings are held, and commitments are remade. Momentum is noticeably lower and skepticism higher. However, the organization can break out of this vicious cycle of change management by embracing the Process of Commitment-Based Change.

Path 2: The Process of Commitment-Based Change

Creating a brand-centric organization is never a perfectly smooth process. No matter how committed the senior leaders, well-thought-out the strategy, or high the degree of organizational buy-in, breakdowns will happen. However, after shepherding nearly 100 of these change-management projects in everything from small businesses to Inc. 500 firms to Fortune 1000 companies, I firmly believe a commitment-based approach leads to greater results faster and with the fewest problems in implementation.

The opposite of the vicious cycle of change management, this process includes all the areas needed for functional alignment that require real change and rolls them out in a chronological order that builds momentum and commitment. The approach is characterized by:

- A clear understanding of what real cultural change takes
- Ownership of the cultural change process at the very top of the organization
- Participation and buy-in from all parts of the company
- Commitment to real change—not just the appearance of change
- Total alignment and participation from senior management in the change
- Assignment of sufficient resources (time, money, staff) to make the change happen
- A clear, agreed-upon structure to keep the change on track and on purpose
- Strategic use of external expertise to assist with the change process

The actual process itself is fairly simple to follow and involves five phases, as Figure 9.4 shows.

PHASE 1: ENGAGE THE C-SUITE

Let's face it: bottom-up cultural change is as rare as a pink unicorn with purple spots. The reality is that unless people believe their leaders are genuinely committed to becoming brand-centric, no process will go very far. I've seen entire organizational transformation projects brought down

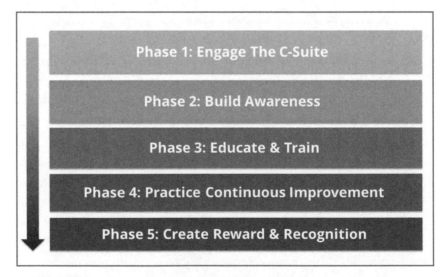

Figure 9.4: **Process of Commitment-Based Change**

by bad behavior on the part of the leadership. Walking the talk is essential to creating a brand-centric organization. Just a few of the actions involved in this first phase of the process include:

- Creating a senior team to oversee the brand-centric cultural change process
- Including a brand-centric focus as an expression of customer commitment in the organizational vision
- Setting long-term and short-term goals for being brand-centric
- Creating and communicating a company-wide message about being brand-centric

PHASE 2: BUILD AWARENESS

In order to gain commitment to the brand-centric process, buy-in must occur within the various levels and constituencies of the organization. Once management commitment is secured, the next step is to assess the gap between the current level of brand-centricity and the desired state. This includes gathering feedback from front-line staff, customers, and management.

PHASE 3: EDUCATE AND TRAIN

The staff who interact daily with your customers are one of your company's greatest brand assets. Having your employees act as brand ambassadors requires educating, training, encouraging, and supporting them. This training can run the gamut: everything from managing online communities to dealing with dissatisfied clients and speaking at public events.

Long-term changes cannot be made in the brand-centric culture of your company without the commitment and support of management, so it's critical to train them in their role as well, including:

- Evaluating their staff's brand-centric attitude and abilities
- Coaching staff in the principles and skills of being brand-centric
- Supporting, encouraging, and rewarding staff for being brand-centric

PHASE 4: PRACTICE CONTINUOUS IMPROVEMENT

It's impossible to create a brand-centric culture without taking on the processes, procedures, systems, and standards at the heart of the way a company does business—both internally and externally.

Continuous brand improvement groups are one of the most efficient and effective ways to deal with this overwhelming tangle of systematic issues. In addition, because they involve staff at all levels and in all areas of the organization, they provide a great opportunity for employee engagement in the process. Later in this chapter you can see a more detailed lay of the land on how you might implement them.

PHASE 5: CREATE REWARD AND RECOGNITION

There are many aspects of an organization's infrastructure that must be addressed to become brand-centric; however, as John E. Jones said, "What gets measured gets done." In the final analysis, what leadership says will only carry as much weight as what it rewards. Financial incentives are only one form of recognizing brand-centric behavior. Creating an environment of recognition is equally powerful. Private and public praise, promotions, acknowledgment, awards, and so on are all part of creating the underlying infrastructure of a brand-centric company culture.

USING THE POWER OF TEAMS TO LIVE THE BRAND

Earlier in this chapter I talked about the need to align processes, procedures, systems, and standards with your brand promise to create a brand-centric company. While there are certainly plenty of issues to explore in the process of becoming brand-centric, the overwhelming nature of this particular arena is one of the main reasons companies fall short in living their brands. It can seem like there is simply too much to do, fix, and change. The deer-in-the-headlights phenomenon takes over, and becoming truly brand-centric as an organization is over before it begins.

Presented with this situation time and again by my corporate clients, I was challenged to find a solution that would have to meet four important criteria:

1. Be relatively easy to implement within an organization.
2. Break the bigger issue of functional alignment and brand promise into smaller, doable chunks.
3. Produce short-term results and long-term impact on living the brand promise.
4. Involve all groups and levels within the organization.

To borrow a line from Dr. Seuss's *How the Grinch Stole Christmas!* (still one of my favorite books, by the way), I puzzled and puzzled till my puzzler was sore—but I came up empty.

Then one day while I was visiting a high-tech client in the Silicon Valley, a heated discussion arose about a brand issue centered on an internal product offering that had been on the table for a year. When I asked why they hadn't just organized a team of people to solve the issue, they said, "Oh, we have had four or five groups take a crack at it, but we can never seem to agree on the solution."

That's when it hit me. Sometimes the right answer is the one that's so close to your face, you can't even see it. In my previous company, I had worked with Inc. 500 and Fortune 500 companies on customer and employee engagement. These initiatives were driven in large part by continuous improvement methods such as quality groups.

The Continuous Brand Improvement Process

I wondered, could a similar methodology (with a few modifications) work for continuous brand improvement? It turns out it could. Using a shorter, more streamlined version of the methodology, I sat down in a room with 15 of the smartest minds in that company, and four hours later, they emerged with a solution to their problem. I knew I'd struck gold. The Continuous Brand Improvement (CBI) Process is a simple methodology any committed company can follow to improve the brand-centric nature of their business and come into functional alignment with their brand promise. The six steps are:

1. Capture all the problems, issues, and concerns.
2. Choose the right problem from the pool of ideas.
3. Select a CBI group facilitator.
4. Bring the CBI group together.
5. Implement the solution.
6. Start all over again.

STEP 1: CAPTURE THE PROBLEMS, ISSUES, AND CONCERNS

One of the most challenging parts of the Continuous Brand Improvement Process is determining which issues, problems, and concerns should be put on the table, and when.

To start, you need a way to capture the majority of issues (big and small) from throughout the organization. The simplest way to do this is to put out a call far and wide for members of the company to propose problems that need solving using a confidential online form. The problems, once received, should be assigned to one of the following five categories of alignment between the brand and the everyday way the organization behaves and functions:

1. Customer experience
2. Management commitment
3. Employee engagement
4. Processes, procedures, systems, and standards
5. Organizational infrastructure

STEP 2: CHOOSE THE RIGHT PROBLEM FROM THE POOL OF IDEAS

Management usually makes the final determination as to which specific problem a particular Continuous Brand Improvement (CBI) group will take on. However, it's worth creating a selection committee to assess the ideas and recommend the problems they feel represent the biggest disconnects in the brand promise.

One suggestion: Start small and work your way up. You want the first problems you choose to be relatively easy ones. Coming out of the gate with a win builds momentum and will set you up to solve more difficult and potentially more contentious problems in the future.

STEP 3: SELECT A CBI GROUP FACILITATOR

After a problem is chosen, and before an official CBI group is gathered, an in-house facilitator is selected. Their job will be to guide the group through the problem-solving process, encourage participation from all group members, and bring in outside resources to provide insight into the problem. It is not their job to proffer their own personal opinions about the problem's causes or solutions. For this reason, it's not necessary for the facilitator to have a hands-on relationship with the problem. I frequently train people within organizations who have no relationship at all to the problem their group is solving to be CBI group facilitators. There are, however, some qualities I've observed that do make for an effective facilitator:

- Being well-respected by their peers, staff, and manager
- Being open to receiving feedback from others as to what is working and not working
- Having strong interpersonal communication skills
- Being able to put their own point of view about the problem aside
- Being trained in the problem-solving methods the company has decided to use

STEP 4: BRING THE CBI GROUP TOGETHER

Although CBI group members may come from different departments or parts of the organization, those who participate should have a hands-on relationship with the specific problem they're going to solve. With the facilitator's objective guidance, the group brainstorms and evaluates the root causes of the problem and identifies, researches, and recommends implementable solutions. Each group usually has between six and ten members who come together for about six to eight weeks and disband when a solution has been reached and presented to management.

STEP 5: IMPLEMENT THE SOLUTION

The CBI group is primarily responsible for coming up with a solution that can be implemented within the organization. Part of the formal problem-solving process involves determining the following:

- Who will be impacted by this solution?
- What is the relative ease of implementing the solution?
- Is it cost prohibitive?
- Will this solution create another problem?
- Does it conflict with another solution we have in place already?

Because this process is so thorough, it's unusual for the group's proposed solution not to be accepted. As for who is responsible for implementation, that varies depending on the nature of the solution and the company. In some cases, the CBI group continues on with the implementation, but in most cases, it's assigned to a third party, who's responsible for seeing the solution through to fruition.

STEP 6: START ALL OVER AGAIN

Kaizen is the Japanese term for continuous improvement, and it is essentially defined as "an ongoing effort to improve products, services, or processes. These efforts can seek 'incremental' improvement over time or 'breakthrough' improvement all at once."

As the name implies, the nature of the Continuous Brand Improvement Process is ongoing. If you continue along this path, you will reach a point when you will have solved many of the core issues facing your company. That said, it's the nature of work that problems will always bubble to the surface that need to be addressed. The process of aligning your brand promise with the way your organization functions is, in many ways, never ending. By putting the Continuous Brand Improvement Process in place, you ensure that you are creating a brand-centric organization—now and in the future.

BEYOND TEAM BUILDING TO TEAM BRANDING

Personal, CEO, and small-business branding are all hot topics today. But there is another type of branding that I've found to be incredibly useful that has not yet made its way into the mainstream—team branding.

Beyond traditional team building or CBI groups, team branding involves helping a defined, intact team (or group brought together for a specific project) define its brand and then translate it into strategy, code of conduct, and action.

Done right, it can have a powerful impact on a team's alignment, effectiveness, and engagement with each other—and the rest of its organization. New and improved team skills are almost always required to make the team brand a reality and, as such, challenge a team to grow in their personal and team talents.

To begin with many teams have never considered the idea that they have a "brand" separate from their organization or department at large.

Taking a step back to proactively generate a specific brand for your intact or project team is the first step in creating a team brand. One effective way to do this is to have an off-site solely designed for the purpose of generating the team's brand. I've been doing these team branding off-sites for years with clients. Here are some of the common reasons to consider having your team generate its own brand:

- If your team needs a deeper alignment and commitment to the current team/project strategic direction
- If your team desires closer relationships between team members and a clearly defined code of conduct
- If your team wants renewed inspiration and engagement with the team, project, or departmental purpose
- If a resolution of ongoing issues/disagreements about team/project direction is needed
- If an acknowledgment of and commitment to personal changes among the members is required to implement the team or project mission
- When you are forming a new project or intact team and/or have had a change in a major team players and need to create alignment on purpose, objectives, and strategy

Borrow from Traditional Brand Building

There's no need to reinvent the wheel here. The way you would go about crafting a brand for a business or even a personal brand is similar to how you create a team brand. A few key questions the group needs engage in include:

- For an established team: Where do we stand today in terms of our brand and reputation in the organization as a whole, and what do we want it to be?
- Where are the gaps?
- What are the short- and long-term impact our team wants to make? What team brand would required to get us there?
- What is our unique branding proposition as a team?

- How will we relate to each other? What principles, values, and commitments do we want to stand for in our team and in the organization as a whole?
- What are the milestones and metrics we will measure ourselves by to ensure that our brand translates into action?

Once generated the team brand can serve as a backdrop for making choices and guiding behavior.

Get Your Team Talking Points Straight

Representing the team to the rest of the organization may involve speaking about the team values, commitment, mission, goals—in short its brand. A well-crafted elevator speech for the team and/or its team project brand that everyone uses when needed will create a consistency of message.

Translate the Team Brand into Action

The point of the team brand is not to print it out on a nice poster and place it on a wall in the break room. The idea is to have the team brand improve team skills and increase effectiveness. One critical way to do this is to make sure the team brand gets translated into action. In the wake of a new team brand, I always ask my clients to revisit their current strategic plan for the following:

- Given our team brand, do any of the items on our strategic plan need to be adjusted, deleted, or changed?
- Given our team brand, do any items need to be added to our current strategic plan?
- What changes will we need to make as a team and as individuals to infuse our team brand into our current strategic plan and objectives?

Market the Team Brand

I'm not a huge fan of your team running out and announcing the team brand to the entire organization—I'm more of a show um, don't tell sort of gal. However, I do think it's essential that your team decide how it will get the message out to the rest of the organization about the team brand.

As one vice president of marketing for a top ten high tech company said, "We here in the marketing department are very bad at marketing the marketing department." Some of the ways leaders have successfully but tastefully "marketed" their team brands to the rest of their organization include:

- Creating an internal customer survey or panel to engage on topical issues, using the event as an opportunity to discuss the team brand
- Writing about the team brand and team brand projects in a company newsletter
- Using internal social media channels to provide mini-moments that keep the message of the team brand alive
- Inviting colleagues from outside the team to visit and give their unique perspective and information on the team project, goal, or strategy)

As with any other brand, your team brand is likely to evolve over time. Changes in your organization, the market, and team players can all influence the need to pivot and adjust the team brand. A yearly one-day off-site just for the purpose of team branding and staying current is a good way to keep your team brand and team skills from getting stale.

CHAPTER TEN

At the Crossroads Where Business and Personal Brands Meet

Why Proactive Career Management
Is a Win for Everyone

Recently a high-powered marketing manager called and told me she was in need of consulting to brush up on her personal brand and prepare for a job interview she had coming up in New York.

In reviewing her resume, I saw that her history was stellar and her credentials were crazy good—not to mention she looked like a well-put-together professional who could make anything happen. I wondered why she needed me.

"I just want to make sure I'm presenting my personal brand as powerfully as I can, so I'm as competitive as possible," she responded. As it turns out, even those at the top of their professional game know that an up-to-date, well-polished personal brand is a distinct advantage when it comes to job interviewing and career management.

As employers gain almost unlimited access via the internet to our personal histories, they also develop a greater demand for details about who we are beyond our business acumen—and they know where to find it.

GET YOUR SOCIAL MEDIA INTERVIEW READY

Calling all recent college graduates, job seekers, midcareer professionals, those desiring a promotion, and second-career candidates: Your future employer wants to know what kind of shape your social media is in.

According to a 2015 CareerBuilder poll, 52 percent of employers use social networking sites to research candidates. If you're not on social media? Too bad, because 35 percent of those same employers reported they were less likely to interview job candidates who didn't have an online presence. In addition, 51 percent use search engines to dig up details on a job candidate.

By the way, sometimes they are sneaky about it. CareerBuilder reported that 35 percent of employers have sent friend requests to potential job candidates with private accounts, and 80 percent who've tried say they've succeeded.

"Researching candidates via social media and other online sources has transformed from an emerging trend to a staple of online recruitment," said Rosemary Haefner, the company's chief human resources officer, in a news release. "In a competitive job market, recruiters are looking for all the information they can find that might help them make decisions."

THE QUALITY OF YOUR DIGITAL FOOTPRINT COUNTS

It's not just being online that matters but the quality of your digital footprint as well. That same CareerBuilder study found that 48 percent of employers chose not to hire a candidate based on their social media content. The most common reasons given for knocking a potential employee out of the running, in descending order, were:

- Provocative or inappropriate photographs
- Information about candidate drinking or using drugs
- Candidate bad-mouthed previous company or fellow employee

- Poor communication skills
- Discriminatory comments related to race, religion, gender, etc.

What Might Get You the Job?

On the flip side, 32 percent of those same employers said they also found content on social sites that made them more likely to hire someone, including, in descending order:

- Candidate's background information supported job qualifications.
- Candidate's personality came across as a good fit with company culture.
- Candidate's site conveyed a professional image.
- Candidate had great communication skills.
- Candidate was creative.

How can you be sure to show these fine qualities on the information superhighway? To begin with, do all the exercises and follow all the recommendations in this book. Doing so will put you in a proactive career management position. For the sake of convenience, however, here's a roundup, in random order, of the ten personal-brand best practices proffered throughout this book.

1. Clarify and articulate your personal brand assets.
2. Rewrite your bio to be bold, not boring, and consider creating a visual CV.
3. Get your LinkedIn profile up to speed.
4. Create a consistent look and feel among all your social media sites and your website (if you have one).
5. Sign up for Google Alerts.
6. Clean up your online presence.
7. Decide on a basic brand-building strategy, and implement it.
8. Get a new headshot.
9. Choose your color palette (if you don't already have one), and design a customized background for all your social media sites and your website (if you have one).
10. Create your brand sound bites.

Weird and Wacky Does Not Win the Day

Employers also shared with the CareerBuilder team some of the oddest pieces of information they had run across on social media for current and potential employees. These included profiles where the person posted a photo of a warrant for his arrest, included links to an escort service, posted dental exam results, bragged about driving drunk and not getting caught, posted Sasquatch pictures he had taken, and featured a pig as his best friend.

Hint: Don't do any of the above.

PROTECT YOUR PRIVACY

Even if you aren't sharing your Sasquatch pictures on Facebook, oversharing is never a good idea. Use the privacy settings on your social media to share posts only with friends and family, never put your address on a site, and consider keeping separate personal and business sites. Oh, and while you're at it, you may want to turn off the tagging options for photos on Facebook. This way no pics of you partying end up with your name attached to them.

CURATE YOUR FRIENDS

When I first started using Facebook, if someone reached out to friend me, I pretty much accepted them without much thought. Then I started getting some questionable messages and weird wall comments. After that, I started hitting the "unfriend" button pretty hard and became much more selective about whom I choose to connect with.

Remember, your personal brand on social media is just as much a matter of who's in your circle as what you choose to post. The goal is to build a network of like-minded individuals with whom you would feel comfortable sharing a mix of appropriate personal and professional information.

TURNABOUT IS FAIR PLAY

Employers aren't the only ones using social media to weed out and let in potential prospects. These same employees are also checking out their would-be future bosses. Another 2015 survey from CareerBuilder found that 15 percent of workers check out hiring managers on social media, with 38 percent of that group seeking to directly interact with them.

WE HAVE COME FULL CIRCLE

Which really brings this whole brand conversation we have been having full circle. Companies want to be the employer of choice and have their pick of the best and brightest out there. Job candidates want to be part of highly regarded, well-run companies where they can shine. Every CEO and executive wants the kind of reputation that raises stock price, adds value to their companies overall, garners them admiration, and puts them on the map as a thought leader. Top people want to work for someone they respect and trust. The bottom line is that everyone wins when brands are at their best—be they business, team, or personal brands.

About the Author

Karen Tiber Leland is the president of Sterling Marketing Group, a branding and marketing strategy and implementation firm that helps CEOs, executives, and entrepreneurs build stronger personal, team, and business brands, and become thought and industry leaders.

In addition, Karen works with startup founders, high-end entrepreneurs, and Fortune 1000 executives in the United States, Europe, and Asia to develop leadership presence through personal branding, team branding, and high-performance productivity. Her clients include LinkedIn, AT&T, Apple, American Express, Cisco, Johnson & Johnson, Marriott Hotels, Oracle, and Twitter.

She is the bestselling author of nine books, which have sold more than 300,000 copies and been translated into ten languages. Karen is a sought-after speaker and has keynoted for hundreds of conferences and associations, including the Young Presidents' Organization, the American Management Association, Harvard, Stanford, and the Direct Marketing Association. She has been interviewed by *The New York Times*, *Fortune*, *Inc.*, *Oprah*, *Bloomberg News*, *Today*, Fast Company, CNN, and *The Wall Street Journal*.

As a freelance journalist, Karen has written articles for *Self*, *Woman's Day*, *American Way*, the *Los Angeles Times*, and others. She regularly writes for Entrepreneur.com, Forbes.com, and others.

In addition to her work in the business world, Karen has worked as an actress and has experience doing industrial films and voiceovers as well as performances on stages throughout the Bay Area and Los Angeles. She is also an exhibiting mixed-media artist and photographer whose work has appeared in group shows in the Museum of Fine Arts in Boston and the Triton Museum of Art in Santa Clara, as well as other venues.

LOOKING FOR MORE HELP IMPLEMENTING YOUR PERSONAL, BUSINESS, OR CEO BRAND?

If you are interested in hiring Karen for your business, team, or personally, there are a variety of ways you can work with her on your branding and marketing strategy and implementation, including the following.

Keynote Presentations

Karen is available for a variety of keynote presentations and break out sessions on the topics covered in this book including:

- The marketing mastery pyramid: design, build, and accelerate your brand
- Personal branding as a path to leadership presence
- Three steps to thought leadership
- Creating your C-Suite and CEO brand
- Building the brand-centric company

Rent My Brain Session

This is a one-hour, lightning-strike strategy session to help you determine the next key action steps in building your brand. It begins with a review of all your online and social media collateral and concludes with an in-depth call to discuss findings and make recommendations.

The Brand Mapping Process

This one-day program takes you (or your team) through an appreciative inquiry process to deeply define your business, team, or personal brand and develop a strategy for brand building over the next 6 to 12 months. Perfect for individuals and organizations looking for greater brand clarity, rebranding or those wanting to get started on the right foot.

Thought Leadership, Executive Presence C-Suite, and CEO Branding

In this 6- to 12-month customized program, Karen works one-on-one with private clients as their "brand manager," helping them design and implement a strategy for establishing their executive presence, thought leadership, and personal brand within their organization and/or the world at large.

Small-Business Branding

Most experts, entrepreneurs, and small-business owners are so busy working in their day-to-day business that they don't have the time or knowledge needed to do the branding and marketing required to build their business. In this intensive 3- to 6-month process, Sterling Marketing Group provides you with the front-end consulting and back-end implementation needed to get your message out to the public, preferred potential customers, and targeted media. Projects are customized based on your unique needs and objectives.

Team Branding

This one-day, off-site session provides intact and project teams with a forum for addressing the default team brand culture they have had in the past, creating a deeper insight into the desired team brand culture of the future, and fostering total support and buy-in for the next level of team brand expression. Follow-up sessions are available as part of the process.

Online Presence Face-Lift for LinkedIn, Twitter, and Other Social Media

The process begins with a detailed review of all your online assets (website, LinkedIn, Twitter, etc.) followed by a call to suggest changes. Once the modifications are agreed upon, your key social media profiles on LinkedIn, Facebook, and Twitter are updated to position your brand and reflect social-media-branding best practices.

Online Branding and Marketing Modules

If you are looking to get the information Karen provides to her private clients at a fraction of the cost, "The Small Business Branding Blowout and Marketing Mastery" online program is ideal. Composed of 15 online, self-led modules, the program takes you through every aspect of marketing and branding you need to build your brand and position yourself.

For more information on these and additional services, or to book Karen Tiber Leland to speak at your next event, please contact Karen@karenleland.com or visit www.karenleland.com.

Index